Forex Day Trading Exposed
Broker Secrets and Winning Strategies Revealed

J.T. WELLESLEY

Contents

PREFACE

In the past decade, I've managed private capital as a full-time trader and I've worked on the dealing desk of a retail foreign exchange ("Forex") brokerage firm. You might say I've done battle on both sides of the fence, and I've long harbored a desire to straighten out many of the misconceptions about the business, an industry that's affected the lives of millions around the world in one way or another.

Trading is a difficult business. And it's made harder not only by the plethora of marketing material generated by salesmen who've never set foot on a trading floor, but also by internet users who give advice - sometimes with the best of intentions... and other times, simply pretending to know more than they really do. Misinformation about the foreign exchange industry is widespread, to say the least, and in some cases, the misconceptions can paint an even worse picture than the truth.

If you've been in the business of trading financial instruments of any kind, for any amount of time, you should already be more than familiar with the challenges that this occupation entails. If not - if you're just starting out - then you'll be more than familiar with these challenges soon enough.

You might've heard that the odds are stacked against you as an individual trader. You might've even heard that people out there are starting to hate you, to demonize you, "the speculators" of the world. After all, when times are tough, it's easy for politicians and the media to assign you the position of collective scapegoats for problems they have no way to solve. What they refuse to acknowledge, of course, is that the individual speculator - the trader - is a person engaged in the epitome of a self-made profession. It's a means for the pursuit of the American dream. No matter where you came from, or who you are, you have the opportunity to control your own fate. And, in this pursuit, you have no one to blame but yourself for both your successes and your failures. For that reason alone, you deserve more respect than the mainstream will afford you in the remaining years of economic crisis.

In my professional experience at a retail currency brokerage firm, my job was to keep an eye on client order flows and, if necessary, manually hedge the exposures that the customers' aggregate positions imposed on the company. In effect, the company's dealing desk not only operated as a proprietary trading unit for the company by making trades on occasion, but it also decided if and when to take the opposite side of the trades coming in from customers. While the practice immediately appears unethical at first glance, this was among the companies that did not directly interfere with the customers' ability to close their trades in profit. In effect, the company simply decided whether to take the risk of maintaining a position opposite certain customers' positions.

Many of the darker truths behind the marketing

hype in the retail Forex industry, and the finance industry at large, make for sensational news and media coverage. After all, what's more likely to sell a book or magazine? Details about a fully compliant firm; or the juicy reveal of law-breaking company that feeds the public's thirst for blood? The truth is often a spectrum of gray areas, far less dramatic than media coverage might imply.

I recall the profit and loss statistics of the clients at the time. Traders on the internet often regurgitate the old statistic, "95% of all traders fail." I could go on forever about some of the impractical assumptions that such a statement implies about any given individual, but what's more important is that the profitability numbers we saw on a daily basis simply did not reflect this 95 percentage loss figure. And the client profitability statistics released by many of the company's peers in recent years have confirmed my observations.

While I aim to be fair in discussing each of the topics that will be covered in this book, I'll note that due to the nature of the details I might reveal along the way, I trust that you'll understand my rationale for not naming specific retail brokerage companies related to particularly sensitive topics mentioned. Before my peers in the industry jump all over it, I should also mention that the truths revealed in this book should also help to clear up some of the overly pessimistic assumptions and accusations made by parties on the outside. In some cases, things simply are not as bad as they seem to people who only know fractions of the truth.

This book is not about attacking or defending any particular industry members. This book is also not about echoing the pessimism spread by struggling traders on the internet. As in many other areas, the truth is between the extremes.

First and foremost, what this book *is* about is the mindset and the methods to improve and grow as an individual trader.

In my time as a Forex dealer, I also began to see the contrasts between the winning and losing strategies employed by traders. I've also immersed myself in the material available to retail traders out of a personal fascination, and I fully understand the challenges that you face in an industry bombarded by misinformation.

Even the most well-meaning of contributors to online FX trading communities occasionally spread misinformation. This is partly because they learned it from unreliable sources, and partly because their own development as a trader is often times based on narrow and dogmatic roots.

You'll find that many of the lessons you'll learn as a trader will apply to other walks of life. Always question your assumptions. Never accept anything as fact without considering the alternatives. In fact, I invite you to question everything in this book. At the worst, you'll have separated yourself as an individual.

I've come to wholeheartedly respect all of you who embark on the challenging journey as a trader in the financial markets. Whether you're already a profitable trader or you're still struggling to turn your trading around, it's my hope that this book will guide you onto the road to realizing your full potential in the world of Forex.

This book includes a number of sample Custom Indicators and tools coded in the MetaTrader 4 programming language, "MQL4". While the MetaTrader platform has many known weaknesses, it undeniably remains one of the most stable and popular software packages offered by the vast majority of retail Forex brokers/dealers worldwide. Plus, it's unanimously available for free before live accounts are opened as brokers offer its full version to download and use for risk-free demo accounts on Windows computers as well as mobile operating systems. A huge library of documentation and free code is also available for its MQL language. After much debate, I chose to provide the code samples in this book using MQL4 for its sheer accessibility.

To use any of the MQL4 code samples in this book, simply install any broker's edition of MetaTrader 4 then go to the Tools drop-down menu inside of the software and click on "MetaQuotes Language Editor". (Alternatively, press the F4 key to launch the editor.) Once the MQL Editor window is open, use the wizard to start a new custom indicator. You may then copy the code from this book exactly as shown and click on "Compile". It should become available in your MetaTrader installation's Navigator window under "Custom Indicators" alongside the software's built-in example custom indicators.

This is also an opportunity to learn the MQL4 language and eventually design your own tools using it or other related programming languages.

CHAPTER 1
CHOICE & MARKET EXPOSURE

For a number of reasons that spanned from convenience to sheer unethical intentions, the early generation of Forex brokers that opened the doors of this market to retail traders were primarily structured to bet against their customers. It originated as a matter of practicality. There was simply no other way to give small traders access to the over-the-counter spot currency market without acting as counterparty. And as it became obvious that the vast majority of that first generation of retail FX traders were nowhere near profitable, it became a simple matter of economics.

Imagine that you were among the first generation of Forex brokers who opened the industry up to retail traders. Early on, you quickly noticed (especially at the time) that the vast majority of your customers were losing their money consistently. With very little regulation at the time, and no limits to the leverage offered, there was simply nothing that stopped you from taking advantage of this. Even without interfering in the trader's ability to win a trade, consider the choice between pocketing one or two pips (in a spread mark-up) per trade, or pocketing hundreds or thousands from a customer's entire account loss. A loss that was all but inevitable.

While this is a bit of a simplification of the bigger picture at the time, it should illustrate the practical reason for the practice.

From an objective standpoint, as long as the broker was not artificially manipulating the price feed for each trader, the practice itself of taking the other side of customers' trades isn't a direct attack on a customer. It's a trade in and of itself, for the company's own books - technically carrying its own risks. After all, every trade in every market is always going to involve a counterparty of some sort. Of course, this is the purely objective and hypothetical theory. In reality, the lack of regulatory oversight at the time triggered far more devious practice, including altering price feeds to specific customers to lean toward their stop loss orders; artificially widening spreads to hit stop losses or margin calls; and other similar practices to "artificially" cause customer losses. By the nature of Forex, as an over-the-counter market, some of these practices were only a matter of bending the rules to the very edge. But when off-shore brokers resorted to refusals to pay out customer profits, they stepped into a whole other level of ethical boundaries.

Fortunately, the industry - as well as its regulatory framework, at least in most of the world's developed countries - has matured quite a bit since then. Refusals of withdrawals are far more rare as long as the broker is properly regulated by a trusted body. And price stream manipulations are becoming far less common as traders learn to watch multiple trading platforms to confirm their pricing feeds.

In the so-called "real" interbank Forex market, prices are determined by the market interaction of large, top-tier financial institutions such as Barclays and UBS participating on electronic information networks that aggregate their pricing. As you might have already learned, Forex is an over-the-counter market which simply means that there is no centralized exchange for currency trading. While that's true, the pricing on the Reuters and EBS systems effectively keep the prices in line with each other. Since the top tier banks only deal in large trades, the retail brokers are typically clients of prime brokerage firms who are themselves clients of these top tier banks.

In effect, the top tier banks are rightfully considered the "real" FX market, where nothing smaller than 10 Standard Lots would typically be traded. (That's 1,000,000 units of base currency, or $100 per pip of movement on a major pair such as EUR/USD.)

Since the beginning of the retail Forex industry, individual traders have been (rightfully) taught to risk no more than 2% of their account per trade. And when the retail Forex brokers opened their online doors to individual traders around the world, a one million unit trade size would be far too large for a retail trader's risk tolerance. Rather than continually raising the leverage available to traders (which would only increase the risk of ruin for small accounts), brokers began to offer smaller trade sizes. At first, Mini Lots (10,000 units or $1 per pip) were offered, later followed by Micro Lots (1,000 units, $0.10 per pip.) Some even offered Nano Lots (100 units, $0.01 per pip) to accommodate smaller accounts who preferred to position trade the market. One particular broker even began to allow their customers to trade individual units of currency, effectively giving Forex the same granularity as individual shares of a stock - allowing traders to size trades accurately to a specific percentage of risk on their account.

This was all well and good... except for one problem. The "real" interbank Forex market would never accept trades smaller than a Standard Lot back then, let alone Mini Lots and smaller.

The solution for retail brokers? (The ones that actually attempted to act as a real middleman between their customers and the interbank market, that is.) Aggregate the small sub-Standard Lot trades on their own books, called a "B-Book", and only pass the equivalent trade to their liquidity providers ("A-Book") when the net exposure is large enough to be traded on the interbank market.

To clarify, that means they were effectively taking the other side of their customers' trades, at least at first (if a trader buys a mini lot and the retail broker is unable to route that trade anywhere, the broker owes its own money if the trade gains and vice versa.) Initially, it sounds like an incredibly shady practice - and, in some cases, it was - but for the more upstanding companies trying to do the right thing, it was simply the only way to handle individual traders' tiny trade sizes in an environment where the interbank market simply had no interest in pocket-change order flow.

With the predominantly uneducated trading

public, it wasn't surprising that the initial generation of retail traders were comprised mostly of amateurs with minimal knowledge of the market, armed with self-destructive gambling tendencies. It was simply far too tempting for many of the retail brokers at the time to simply B-Book all of their traders, or at least the groups that appeared to be consistently losing.

Of course, not every trader would consistently lose, so many retail brokers simply had to cover their own exposure, regardless of their own standards of ethics and morality. The common practice for brokers who offered Mini Lots and other smaller trade sizes to retail traders was to aggregate all of those smaller trades at any given time into an X number of Standard Lots of the currency pair, and then "hedge" their own exposure by placing that X number of Standard Lots as a trade on the same currency pair with their prime broker - who then may cover their own exposure the same way with the top tier banks, and so on.

There are two issues that this practice should inform individual traders of.

Firstly, not all retail traders are consistently losing anymore. Sometimes, not even a majority. If the majority were consistently losing, none of the retail brokers would ever have to hedge their own exposure.

Secondly, the net effect of a large group of individual traders can, in fact, make some extent of impact on the interbank Forex market... but only when a very, very large majority of these traders are on the same side of a particular trade. (It doesn't happen every day, but it does happen.)

From the traders' perspective, netting smaller trades was a compromise for gaining access to a market that was once almost entirely exclusive to a small circle of the financial elite. And as technology advanced, retail brokers began to build automated or semi-automated systems to control the company's risk exposure.

In some cases, brokers may choose not to hedge their own exposure to certain traders. For instance, if a particular trader has a solid record of losing trades, it makes economic sense for the broker to hold this trader's positions on its own books in order to profit from the trader's losses. This is a choice that comes with its own risks, just as much as the trader's own positions are his or her choices with inherent risks.

As retail traders became increasingly savvy of the brokers' practices, the companies that engaged in questionable practices either had to adapt to survive, or risk losing their customers and reputations to growing competitors.

Additionally, as financial regulations began to tighten, many of the larger retail brokers registered under strict regulators that would scrutinize their practices and impose fines for many of these violations. Today, many retail Forex brokers have moved away from these forms of blatantly unethical operations to some extent, if not altogether. The safest bet for individual traders is to choose a well capitalized and well regulated company that's established a reputation among professional individual traders.

The unethical practices of the early generation of retail Forex brokers only emphasized the youth of the retail industry. After all, it's often called the Wild West of financial markets. As this sub-industry matured in recent years, these underhanded practices are becoming less of a concern for individual traders.

Instead, what you should take from this is that your broker has always had less of an inherent advantage than it may appear at first glance.

As long as your broker can't simply refuse to pay out withdrawals to profitable traders without consequences (and there would be consequences if they're registered with any legitimate regulatory body), choosing not to cover their exposure to your trades is not a risk-free venture on their end. The practice of B-Booking a trader's trades is as risky for the company as the trade is for the trader, less the spread as an inherent (and small) edge.

As a simplified example, recall that some individual traders might strictly adhere to trend-following strategies taught by the typical online education course. Many will fail to stick to the discipline taught by these courses, but a small minority might really succeed at it. As a result, this minority will exhibit a profitability pattern that begins with a long streak of relatively small losses - a streak long enough to make him or her look like a prime candidate to be B-Booked... And then, a single, rare, but much larger gain wipes out all of the trader's losses and more.

In October 2008, the USD/CAD broke out and trended almost 2,500 pips with no significant retracements to speak of. While the same breakout traders may have steadily lost small amounts up until that move, the move itself was more than enough for the most disciplined of those traders to catch the majority of the gains... and for some retail brokers to make unexpected losses. This is one of the reasons that trend trading is among the most difficult strategies, but also one that a broker should not bet against.

While it was rare to find these sorts of traders grow into a majority of a company's customers, it's only one example of the types of traders who can unexpectedly turn the tables. So B-Booking is never a risk-free venture.

To aid in understanding the broker's point of view, I've designed an exercise. The goal of this exercise is not to convince you that ethically-questionable retail Forex dealers deserve undue sympathy. The goal is to train you to understand your potential opposition; and to understand some of the ways you can still win or at least gain a more objective point of view about the practices.

Whether a broker employs a dealing desk or

runs an automated system that it may occasionally override, every broker must prevent the company's own exposure to customers' winning trades - typically trades that are sub-Standard Lot in size - from growing into significant losses. And when this net exposure comes from hundreds of customers in one way or another, the firm is effectively scaling in and out of positions continuously. Worse yet, unlike the trader's point of view, these trades are established by the free will of people outside of their control.

In this exercise, you'll need two demo accounts. Practically every retail Forex broker offers demo trading accounts for free. In general, they're only really effective as demonstrations of the software platform itself, and the speed of the company's network connections to your internet provider. In this case, a demo account is all you'll need for the exercise.

Do NOT try this with live accounts.

Once you've opened two demo accounts, familiarize yourself with the trading platform if you haven't already. The nuances of the software shouldn't be alien to you. Two brokers who offer MetaTrader are fine for this exercise since MetaTrader runs perfectly on most Windows computers when multiple instances of it are running simultaneously. (If you're on a Mac or Linux, a number of brokers also offer Java-based trading software.)

During the first hours of a major Forex market

session (typically the hour before the stock market opens in major financial centers such as London, New York, or Tokyo) watch for the first large move of the day on your favorite major pair (GBP/USD, EUR/USD, USD/JPY, USD/CHF, AUD/USD, USD/CAD). This first relatively large move will obviously vary from day to day - it's typically smaller on Mondays or at quiet times of year - but will likely become more volatile than the hours that preceded the session open. It'll also, often times, break the high or low of the previous regional banking session.

Let's call this the first breakout of the day, when price breaks out of a short-term range and triggers many trend-following breakout traders to jump in on a new trend.

If it broke downward, sell to open a short position on the first demo account. If it broke upward, buy to open a long position on the first demo account.

Every trade you open on the first demo account, open the exact opposite trade on the second demo account at roughly the same time (as quickly as possible.) No stop loss order. No take profit order.

You might have all sorts of preconceived notions about where you think price will go, or whether you think this move "should" happen, but there's nothing you can do about the exposure you just took. Remember, you're a retail broker in this exercise's second demo account. You can't choose the initial trades; your hypothetical customers did. And in this case, it's a large group of breakout traders that you're exposed to.

As the market moves, decide where you want to cover your exposure in the second demo account. (To cover, simply close the trade in your trading software. Imagine that this action is you placing the customers' aggregated trade size through to your retail broker's prime brokerage.)

For the next week, repeat this exercise every day at the open of the same session and keep watching the market. Look for areas where you can scale out of your position (reducing the exposure of yourself as a retail broker.) Just watch the price action and try to exit your exposure at the smallest loss possible, or maybe even a small profit. Don't think in terms of stop losses and take profit orders. Just think in terms of overall exposure to the market between both accounts.

After a week, start trading in the first demo account from the mindset of a regular trader, and continue to take the opposite positions on the second demo account. Having watched price action for a week, you should have some idea of where you think the best entries are. Have they improved?

If not, repeat the broker point-of-view exercise.

The point of this exercise is not only to gain a better perspective of retail Forex brokers, but also to force you to watch the market from two different points of view. For every buyer, there's a seller out there that took the opposite side for one reason or another. Even if the opening of one party's trade is the closing of the other, both parties are watching the same price levels and strategizing on when to add and remove exposure. Practicing the ability to see price levels from both points of view will improve your objectivity about the way the market moves. (The speed, the size of trends, the way price levels stall a trend, etc.)

Remember, no matter how much larger the broker is than you are, it's you - the customer - who is in control of the first step of trade entry. As long as you choose a broker that's registered with a legitimate regulatory body, there's only so much as the broker can do to avoid paying out your profits within legal boundaries.

Acknowledge your control - this is important. Leave the politicians and the media to resorting to scapegoats. Take responsibility for your trades, and you'll improve as a trader.

Of course there are parties who oppose your interests. So what? In every industry, in every line of work, there will always be a party that opposes your interests in one way or another. You can't let that stop you cold. It should motivate you to strike fear in your opposition, and move them out of the way of your success.

After all, it's your move.

CHAPTER 2
RANDOMNESS & MARKET MOVERS

At the two extremes, there are two schools of thought on the financial markets: Those who believe that the market is nothing but a random walk, and those who believe there are secret patterns to be discovered. Most people who participate in any given market fall somewhere in the middle but some will harbor a deeper belief in the random walk theory as a sort of innate fear. And it's only a fear because many traders believe that if random walk theory is true, then their own pursuit of trading is pointless.

As with most things in life, extremes are rarely accurate from an objective point of view.

In my early years in the finance industry as an institutional trader, I harbored a subconscious fear that the random walk theory was entirely correct. The entire existence of my occupation was predicated on the market being less than entirely random, at the very least. Despite long having known of Nicholas Taleb's book, *Fooled by Randomness* (Random House, 2001), I had put off reading it for years - secretly fearing that the truths his work might expose about the pure randomness of the markets would somehow become truer for me if I had become aware of it. As I grew personally in my trading career, that fear faded away and I made an effort to see things more objectively. And I finally gave it a read. As it turned out, even the well-reasoned arguments Taleb made in his book were not that the markets were entirely random. Only that people often underestimate the role of randomness in both the markets and in life.

After my professional experience at a retail Forex broker, I've never agreed more with his views than I do now.

The market is not 100% random, but it often appears to be.

Sure, you can produce a random walk generated by a computer and it would closely resemble a chart of a financial market. In fact, you might even find trendlines and support and resistance areas on that random walk. The problem is that it's still not the result of the same type of randomness.

To use a metaphor, imagine that there is a school of thought that every automobile on this planet is, in fact, a figment of your imagination that was most likely generated by special effects. A group of strong believers in this theory then produce a Hollywood-caliber computer graphics rendering of a BMW and superimpose it onto the photo of their driveway. They then show you a photo of the same car, which you own, and place it side by side with their computer-generated photo. They look almost indistinguishable even to the most hardcore of car lovers.

Does that really mean BMW doesn't make real cars? They only exist as a special effect?

Sure, a pure random walk chart looks nearly identical to a chart of historical price action on a financial market... but that doesn't prove both images came from the same origins.

Before this reduces to a one-sided tirade against the random walk theory, I do want to acknowledge one caveat.

At many times of day, especially in intraday trading, the price action of any given currency can, in fact, appear largely random for all practical purposes. I say for all practical purposes because there's no known way of capitalizing on them using the information available to the average retail Forex trader.

To resort to another metaphor, let's imagine that someone is blowing a dog whistle in your ear. The dog whistle is, in fact, vibrating the oxygen molecules and therefore, it is producing sound... but only your pets can hear it. You can't.

The "big dogs" in the Forex market - the trading desks at the Barclays and Citigroups of the world - are privy to information on order flows that retail currency traders simply do not have access to. They hear the whistle all the time, and they're simply big enough that when they move, all the other animals in the room will scramble in the same direction. All you can do is watch how they all react to the whistle and guess where the whistle is coming from.

In this way, the net effect of all the capital moving from one party to another (the animals scrambling from one side of the room to the other) will create an effect that appears entirely random to you at times. That's fine. As in every pursuit in life, you can only acknowledge your inherent weaknesses and play on your strengths.

When the big dogs are shuffling back and forth, using information you have no access to, the net effect is an illusion of randomness. Depending on your definition of the term, you might even consider it completely random for all practical purposes from your point of view. All that really matters is that, at times, there really isn't much you can do to capitalize on the price action... but when the right opportunity shows itself, you can use your agility - as a tiny creature - to maneuver your way around the big dogs and claim the tiny leftovers for your relatively smaller stomach.

In other words, as a small individual Forex trader, your strength in the market doesn't come at all times. When it does come, pounce on it and you'll claim your piece of the pie.

In reality, price moves because of a net aggregate of human decisions, and decisions made by automated computer algorithms... designed by people. These decisions are weighted by the money on the line -- but, as mentioned earlier, when a large enough group of individual traders take the same side of the trade, it tends to reach the interbank market in some form simply because the counterparties all the way up the chain need to reduce their own exposure. There is no secret pattern to solve, just human intentions - even if by proxy through a computerized trading system.

When these crowd decisions are relatively balanced, there's very little you can do as an individual trader. When they've reached an imbalance, you have opportunities capitalize on those imbalances.

People who pretend to be experts love to paint the market as being manipulated by one, single almighty entity called "smart money." While it's partly true that the biggest players in the market can move price simply because of the size of their orders, the way these terms are often used infers the wrong mental picture for a beginner trader and will only be destructive to a trader's mindset.

Rather than picturing one powerful monster jerking price back and forth at will, you should instead imagine it as a room full of smaller creatures all trying to pull and push in different directions. Only when more than half of the total mass (the mass being the money value traded by each market participant) of these creatures happen to agree on a direction will price actually move.

You might assume the creatures with the most mass in the room are generally the top tier banking institutions, the too-big-to-fail names in the world's major financial centers, but that's not always the case. Aside from managing their exposure to orders from prime brokerage firms (whose clients include retail Forex brokers), the top tier banks must also handle orders from Corporates and Sovereigns.

Corporates refers to the multi-national corporations such as General Electric or Sony, who must exchange large amounts of currency as part of their cross-border businesses.

Sovereigns are the governments of countries who may be exchanging currencies for any number of reasons. It's no secret in the world of finance that they also purposely manipulate the Forex market at times to their own benefit. (Export-driven economies benefit from lowering their own currency's value, and many countries have engaged in a "currency war" in recent years to devalue their own currencies.)

Corporates' and Sovereigns' entries and exits in the Forex market almost completely disregard the reasons a typical trader (or "speculator") would have to open or close a trade. They also tend to stagger their orders. (Because of the large amounts these parties intend to transact, they can't just buy up or dump their entire trade size at once.) These sorts of trades are visible when you watch live market action, as they tend to stop trends dead with price action struggling and failing to break a zone, or sometimes even triggering a powerful start of a new trend. The distinct motion makes these events are more obvious if you watch the market live rather than scroll through historical data.

Unlike many other participants, the dissemination of their order information is less likely to be detrimental to them. The Corporates tend not to be bothered, having already factored in an acceptable range of loss from foreign exchange transactions. The Sovereigns sometimes even prefer to be seen, especially when their goal is to move the market in their country's economic favor.

As of the time of this writing, Deutsche Boerse's Market News service is one of the few available sources of information on large pending orders in the interbank FX market that is available to individual traders. In any case, traders can also learn to watch for the market reactions to the orders placed by these participants.

Relatively smaller participants (but still gigantic from the perspective of retail traders) include smaller banks, hedge funds, mutual funds, ETFs, and independent proprietary trading firms. While it's generally rare to see a single entity within these categories cause a significant move in the FX market, there are a few big participants within these categories that can snow ball their trades into a noticeable market move.

While there's no real way to tell exactly who is doing what at all times in this market - especially considering the Forex liquidity aggregation systems allow for anonymity - traders should maintain a realistic mental image of who is really likely to be driving the prices behind your charts and quotes. And it's not a random walk generator.

In the vast majority of cases, it makes very little sense for all of these major market participants to band together in some sort of conspiracy to move the market at will. In some cases, many of the participants have conflicting interests with other participants - especially the Sovereigns with export-driven economies.

Here's an example of a scenario that moves prices: Participant A begins accumulating because it either wants to or needs to (to adjust exposure or to gain some for its own accounts); Participant B needs to dump some and sees an opportunity after A drove it up a bit. Result so far: consolidation... until B exhausts the total amount it intended to sell. Now there's very little holding price down if A isn't finished buying. And if no one is hitting A's bids, and it still needs to buy more, its only choice is to buy from the offers at price levels above posted by C. C might be sitting there with offers at higher prices because it plans to open short positions for the long term, or maybe it's just to dump some of their old long positions. Either way, A will have to begin eating away at C's offers if A wants to continue buying. Still, A is able to buy at decent prices, so A decides to buy more... but then boom, C's offers are exhausted. The next offers are above, but they're smaller, so if A continues to buy -- it'll breakout to the upside, fast... until D, a fellow large participant enters with sell orders. D could be a large bank filling its customers orders or maybe a major hedge fund looking to take profits from an existing trade. They stop the upward move, dead.

Still, A's not done, so this isn't even close to a reversal. Instead, retail traders see a pause in the upward move on their charts, maybe a pullback to a Fibonacci retracement level. Will it continue its "trend" upward? Will it fall back down? Will retail traders fall asleep from boredom as it continues to consolidate sideways for another fifteen minutes?

Ultimately, a trader's job is to watch events like this unfold with little to no information on the identity of the participants (or even whether it was one party who drove price up or a whole bunch who happened to piggyback the initial trades). And that detail isn't entirely necessary to profit from these moves. What's necessary is the ability to watch these events unfold and be able to react in a constructive way.

One of the most destructive assumptions to a beginner trader's development is the belief that a secret combination of indicators exists. It's an inherent misunderstanding of the market, and can delay a trader's true development for years if not indefinitely.

Keeping a more realistic mental picture of the market in mind will help a trader manage expectations. You can't accurately predict the decisions of other humans (or human-made computers acting out human intentions.) You can only react in probability driven ways to profit from scenarios you recognize.

Many things in the world will appear random to those who don't fully understand the mechanisms behind it. Just don't forget that your goal as a trader is to bring your own level of understanding to a level well beyond that.

CHAPTER 3
PREDICTABLE DAILY VOLATILITY

The Forex market is routinely referred to as a 24-hour market but that's a distortion of the truth. It runs for five days straight, from Monday at 8AM in Sydney to Friday at 5PM in New York, because the banks' hours in each of the major global financial centers (typically 8AM to 5PM) overlap each other. And not all of those hours are created equal. By assuming they are, you will at the very least be bored to death at certain times of day, and shocked into panic at others.

On the most liquid currency pairs, the major financial centers involved are, in order: Sydney, Tokyo, Frankfurt, London, and New York. These cities are also home to the developed economies with equity (stock) markets that open approximately an hour after the banks begin operations for the day. Approximately 8AM to 10AM in each of these cities' respective time zones will typically be the most volatile periods for the major currency pairs. This is especially true for the first two hours of operation at the banks in London and New York.

The main reason it seems to be so difficult for web sites to get this information entirely right at all times of year is that it's much less straightforward than you would assume at first glance. Firstly, Japan doesn't use Daylight Savings Time, and England has long been considering the end of their use of British Summer Time (their term for Daylight Savings.) Even while England uses it, the dates on which the UK switches to and from BST does not match up with the exact dates when the US switches to and from Daylight Savings. Lastly, Australia also has different Daylight Savings switch dates. And to complicate things further, Australia happens to be in the southern hemisphere, so when everyone else (who uses Daylight Savings at all) is "Springing forward", they're "Falling back" and vice versa, leaving many of the online guides to FX session times inaccurate by an hour for half of the year.

Here's the easiest method to accurately find the start and end times of each financial center's banking hours: Banks in all of these major cities are generally open from 8:00 AM (08:00) to 5:00 PM (17:00) in the respective city's local time zone. By looking up the current time (as of the current date) of each city at any given time, you can better gauge the actual period of expected volatility breakouts of the day.

Why does any of this matter?

Well, momentum traders should only watch the opening hours of London and New York for the big trending moves that present intraday momentum opportunities. Tokyo and Sydney are generally better suited to mean reversion styles of trading as they're relatively range-bound by comparison. For part time traders, an added factor to consider is whether each time zone's prime hours (the first couple of hours of the day in the time zone) overlaps with other obligations. Many part-time traders in North America prefer to specialize in the Sydney and Tokyo sessions for this reason alone, as their opening hours are in the

North American evening.

Don't let the time on your trading platform confuse you further. Many retail brokers use varying time zones on their trading platforms, which has resulted in a mess when it comes to identifying a single standard for daily bars or candles on Forex charts. However, the generally accepting beginning and end to a day is the end of the American bank hours at 5:00 PM ET (New York time). This standard is relatively consistent since it's typically the time of rollovers (when interest differentials - between the currencies in a pair - is charged or credited for open positions.) It's also the end of the entire trading week on Friday before the market re-opens on Monday morning Australian time (Sunday afternoon in New York).

Unfortunately, retail FX charting packages aren't all configured to show this properly so it may be necessary to create custom indicators or other utilities to show the actual daily highs and lows.

As a basis for measuring a currency pair's volatility, you can use Average Daily Range. It's not a built-in feature on some trading platforms but it's one of the easier calculations in almost every platform's programming language... at least in theory.

Since MetaTrader is, for better or worse, the single most popular trading platform among retail FX brokers, I'll mention that there's an easy way to calculate Average Daily Range using MetaTrader regardless of the broker's time zone settings on their servers. Using the MetaTrader MQL (MetaQuotes Language) "iHigh" and "iLow" built-in functions with offset values, you can start with the hour following the NYC close and end with the next day's 4PM New York time bar; find the highest and lowest, and store those values to create your own synthetic daily candle. Obviously, to get the Average Daily Range for the past 21 days, simply sum the differences between those highs and lows and divide by 21. Fortunately, many retail FX brokers choose to use the Central European Time Zone so that the NYC close hour appears conveniently as 00:00 (midnight) so adjustments wouldn't be necessary. It's also likely that ADR would not be significantly thrown off by a few hours shift, but it's always better to be accurate especially when you begin using your data for testing.

Here's our sample code for calculating ADR using the MetaTrader 4 MetaQuotes Language:

```
//MetaTrader 4 MQL code for ADR:

double ADR = 0;
int NumOfDays = 21;
for (int x=NumOfDays;x>0;x--)
{
   ADR += iHigh(Symbol(),PERIOD_D1,x) -
          iLow(Symbol(),PERIOD_D1,x);
}
ADR = ADR / NumOfDays;
Comment("ADR("+NumOfDays+"): "+ADR+"\n");

//End of MQL code for ADR
```

Average Daily Range is an excellent barometer for market intraday conditions because it allows a trader to gauge the amount of volatility to expect within a given trading day within a reasonable estimate. The average taken over a 21 day period is my ADR of choice because 21 is the average number of trading days per month. This is generally a big enough sample size to indicate the current volatility environment and at the same time recent enough to be kept up to date at the time of calculation.

To calculate Average Daily Range manually (or using Excel), simply take the highs and lows of the past 21 days and subtract the low from the high for each day; then sum them all together and divide by 21.

Average True Range (ATR) is a commonly used alternative, but the formula for ATR was originally created for stock prices which exhibit large gaps between daily data by nature. Its calculation purposely used the previous day's close as the next day's open to adjust for gaps between trading days on stock markets. In the Forex market, prices don't gap much, if at all, between days of the same week because there's no real stop and start period in between the overlapping sessions. Its prices are seamlessly continuous between Monday morning in Sydney and Friday afternoon in New York. So the ATR calculation isn't entirely practical as a measure of intraday volatility but will suffice as an alternative if it's within easier access.

The second measure of volatility for intraday

traders is the Average First Hour range. Simply subtract the low from the high of the last 21 sessions' local 8AM to 9AM hour to get the Average First Hour. Obviously, it's possible to find the Average First Hour value for four different sessions but the most practical measures are the ones for London's first hour and New York's first hour. One or both of these should be more than enough to gauge the current environment from the perspective of intraday FX traders.

Another significant reason for keeping track of the intraday sessions is the correlation of currencies with their local stock markets. Due to the nature of currencies (as the instruments used to price stocks) the flow of capital into and out of stocks and commodities will directly affect the strength of a particular currency. To place emphasis on that: the impact will be on the singular currency, not the currency pair directly.

It's also safe to say the US Dollar paired with each of the other liquid currencies would likely be affected nonetheless, but the concept of a single currency's strength relative to the other highly traded currencies is a factor that deserves more attention from serious FX traders.

CHAPTER 4
MEASURING FX CAPITAL FLOWS

Beginner traders tend to gravitate toward one or two currency pairs either because a guru has told them that it's the only pair worth trading, or because some other preconception about the pair makes it particularly attractive. There's nothing entirely wrong with choosing to specialize in a specific instrument - pros often become "surrogate specialists" - but the FX market also offers an additional opportunity to increase your probability of success. And anything, any factor, that increases your probability of success is worth adding to your toolbox for trading in the FX market.

The main pool of currency pairs you should look at are the most heavily traded pairs by turnover volume on a daily basis. While the exact percentages naturally vary in each of the Bank of International Settlements' triennial publications, the top ranked pairs included in the top of the list have remained consistent.

Currency Pairs with Highest Daily Volume

EUR/USD - Euro vs. US Dollar (27-30%)

USD/JPY - US Dollar vs. Japanese Yen (14-20%)

GBP/USD - British Pound vs. US Dollar (9-13%)

AUD/USD - Australian vs. US Dollar (4- 6%)

USD/CAD - US vs. Canadian Dollar (4-5%)

USD/CHF - US Dollar vs. Swiss Franc (4-5%)

(Figures listed are the percentages of total daily average turnover volume in each currency pair over the past decade as reported by the Bank of International Settlements.)

Choosing Currency Pairs to Trade

One of the first tools you should familiarize yourself with is Relative Strength Ranking.

Relative Strength Ranking should not to be confused with the Relative Strength Index (RSI) indicator, which is a lagging technical indicator derived mathematically from the price of only one currency pair. Relative Strength Ranking is a method of comparing the returns of multiple financial instruments and then assigning them a rank based on recent performance.

Its results are a way to gauge the recent flow of capital into and out of specific instruments relative to other instruments in its class. Depending on the nature of the market you're watching, this information is often statistically significant either for continuations or reversals. By using this information at the appropriate times in the FX market, we're able to compare the relative capital flows into and out of specific currencies and currency pairs, and use variations of it to tell us which pairs will be the strongest and weakest pairs to trade in the following day's session.

The variations of Relative Strength Ranking that I'll introduce are two methods which can be used effectively in a layered approach. The first is Currency Strength Rank which focuses on the daily capital flows of each currency (not each currency *pair* but each *individual currency*), and the second is Hourly Relative Strength which instead focuses on the recent intraday capital flows into each currency *pair* (not individual currencies, in this case.)

The purpose of the daily data based Currency Strength Rank is to give traders a broader view of recent capital flows into each of the individual currencies, completely independent of other currencies. The unique aspect of this measurement is that it separates each individual currency into its own performance against the other highly-traded currencies rather than viewing it as a pair as we usually do.

Conversely, with the Hourly Relative Strength, we are simply looking for the most recent hour of capital flows into and out of a particular pair. This is a more "traditional" measurement by FX trading standards as it treats the pair as a single financial instrument. (While some beginners have mistakenly believed that this information is irrelevant, keep in mind that the major interbank market participants do, in fact, transact on major pairs - not individual currencies.) It may seem awfully short-sighted to use only one hour of data for such a measurement, but this tool is best used during the second hour of each financial center's FX trading session up until the lunch hour of the respective time zone. (9AM to Noon in each of the intraday sessions' respective time zones.) The purpose of this method is to see the change in recent movements of capital since the first hour of the session (8AM in the session's time zone) as a gauge of the day's capital flows to and from each of the major pairs.

Combined, Currency Strength Rank and Hourly Relative Strength form a strong multi-currency view point of the market.

They also help traders to see when the broad market is leaning toward greed or fear based on the categories of currencies receiving the most in flows of capital from the FX market's major participants.

The Hourly Relative Strength calculates each currency pair's return in the previous hour as a percentage and then divides it by the Average Daily Range of the past 21 days to output it's movement in the previous hour in the form of a volatility-adjusted value.

Here's a sample output from my custom MetaTrader code example for Hourly Relative Strength:

```
EURUSD: 5.69727526
GBPUSD: 2.63877068
AUDUSD: 12.88932986
USDJPY: 0.07658860
USDCHF: -7.90759263
USDCAD: -12.66058535
```

In the above example output, the pair with the strongest capital inflows in the previous hour was AUD/USD and the weakest was USD/CAD. (Taken on an individual currency level, the AUD and CAD were the strongest while the USD was weak against them.)

The formula for the Hourly Relative Strength factor is ((Previous Hour's Open - Previous Hour's Close) / (Previous Hour's Open) * 100) / (21-Day ADR).

Sample MetaTrader 4 MQL code for an Hourly Relative Strength on-screen display:

```
//Hourly Relative Strength in MQL4

//External variables for the user
extern string prefix = "";
extern string suffix = "";

string Output;
string sym[6] = {"EURUSD", "GBPUSD",
"AUDUSD", "USDJPY", "USDCHF", "USDCAD"};
string brokersym[6];
double symreturn[6];
double ADR[6];
double rankfactor[6];

int init()
  {
   for(int x=0;x<6;x++)
   {
     brokersym[x] = prefix + sym[x] + suffix;
   }
   return(0);
  }

int deinit()
  {
   return(0);
  }

int start()
  {
   Output = "";
   for(int y=0;y<6;y++)
   {
     ADR[y] = 0;
     if (iHigh(brokersym[y],PERIOD_D1,21) > 0
     && iLow(brokersym[y],PERIOD_D1,21) > 0 )
     {
       for(int a=21;a>0;a--)
       {
         ADR[y] +=
```

```
iHigh(brokersym[y],PERIOD_D1,a)
- iLow(brokersym[y],PERIOD_D1,a);
       }
        ADR[y] = ADR[y] / 21;
      }
      if (iOpen(brokersym[y],PERIOD_H1,1) > 0
          && ADR[y] > 0 )
      {
        symreturn[y] =
        ((iClose(brokersym[y],PERIOD_H1,1)
        - iOpen(brokersym[y],PERIOD_H1,1) )
        / iOpen(brokersym[y],PERIOD_H1,1) )
        * 100;
        rankfactor[y] = symreturn[y] / ADR[y];
      }
      else return(0);
      Output = Output + "\n" +
               sym[y] + ": " + rankfactor[y];
    }
    Comment(Output);
    return(0);
  }

//End of MQL4 code
```

The Currency Strength Rank, on the other hand, ranks the most highly traded individual currencies (not currency pairs) based on recent data from the major pairs and their crosses. The returns of major pairs and crosses are also converted into values relative to the pair's 21-day Average Daily Range. Using a multi-period approach, we do this with each pair on a 1-hour, 5-hour and 120-hour time frame (weighted 40%, 30%, 30% respectively.) We then score the strength of each individual currency (for example, if the ADR-adjusted return of EUR/USD was up, then EUR is awarded one point and USD is reduced by one point; conversely, if the EUR/USD returned a negative value, then EUR is reduced by one point and USD is awarded one.) All pairs and crosses are processed this way until we have a resulting score for each individual currency.

An example of the output from my sample MQL4 code for Currency Strength Rank below:

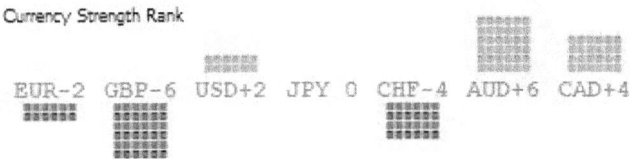

Currency Strength Rank

EUR-2   GBP-6   USD+2   JPY 0   CHF-4   AUD+6   CAD+4

In the example output, AUD (Australian Dollar) was the strongest with the most capital flow into it and GBP (British Pound) was the weakest with the most capital flow away from it. Traders can use this information to choose the GBP/AUD cross as the pair of choice for today's trading session.

Forex Day Trading Exposed

Here's the sample MetaQuotes Language 4 code for Currency Strength Rank which produced the above example output:

```
// Currency Strength Rank in MQL4

extern string prefix =      "";
extern string suffix =      "";

string    Display_Name =    "Currency Strength
Rank";
int       PeriodA =         1;
int       PeriodB =         5;
int       PeriodC =         120;
int       TF =              60;
double    FactorA =         0.40;
double    FactorB =         0.30;
double    FactorC =         0.30;
bool      LimitRefreshes =  true;
int       RefreshSeconds =  3;
bool      Debug =           false;
datetime  TimeLastLoaded;
int       USD, EUR, GBP, CHF, JPY, AUD, CAD;

int init()
  {
   IndicatorShortName(Display_Name);
   return(0);
  }

int deinit()
  {
   int obj_total=ObjectsTotal();
   for(int i=obj_total;i>=0;i--)
   {
      string name= ObjectName(i);
      if(StringSubstr(name,0,6)=="Demand")
       ObjectDelete(name);
   }
   Comment("");
   return(0);
  }

int start()
```

```
   {
   if(TimeCurrent() <
TimeLastLoaded+RefreshSeconds
      && LimitRefreshes == true)
      return(0);

   string EURUSD = prefix+"EURUSD"+suffix;
   string EURGBP = prefix+"EURGBP"+suffix;
   string EURCHF = prefix+"EURCHF"+suffix;
   string EURJPY = prefix+"EURJPY"+suffix;
   string EURAUD = prefix+"EURAUD"+suffix;
   string GBPUSD = prefix+"GBPUSD"+suffix;
   string GBPCHF = prefix+"GBPCHF"+suffix;
   string GBPJPY = prefix+"GBPJPY"+suffix;
   string GBPAUD = prefix+"GBPAUD"+suffix;
   string USDCHF = prefix+"USDCHF"+suffix;
   string CHFJPY = prefix+"CHFJPY"+suffix;
   string AUDCHF = prefix+"AUDCHF"+suffix;
   string USDJPY = prefix+"USDJPY"+suffix;
   string AUDJPY = prefix+"AUDJPY"+suffix;
   string AUDUSD = prefix+"AUDUSD"+suffix;
   string EURCAD = prefix+"EURCAD"+suffix;
   string GBPCAD = prefix+"GBPCAD"+suffix;
   string USDCAD = prefix+"USDCAD"+suffix;
   string CADJPY = prefix+"CADJPY"+suffix;
   string CADCHF = prefix+"CADCHF"+suffix;
   string AUDCAD = prefix+"AUDCAD"+suffix;

   if(ErrorCheck(EURUSD) > 0)
   { PrintErrorMessage(); return(0); }
   if(ErrorCheck(EURGBP) > 0)
   { PrintErrorMessage(); return(0); }
   if(ErrorCheck(EURCHF) > 0)
   { PrintErrorMessage(); return(0); }
   if(ErrorCheck(EURJPY) > 0)
   { PrintErrorMessage(); return(0); }
   if(ErrorCheck(EURAUD) > 0)
   { PrintErrorMessage(); return(0); }
   if(ErrorCheck(GBPUSD) > 0)
   { PrintErrorMessage(); return(0); }
   if(ErrorCheck(GBPCHF) > 0)
   { PrintErrorMessage(); return(0); }
   if(ErrorCheck(GBPJPY) > 0)
   { PrintErrorMessage(); return(0); }
   if(ErrorCheck(GBPAUD) > 0)
   { PrintErrorMessage(); return(0); }
```

```
if(ErrorCheck(USDCHF) > 0)
{ PrintErrorMessage(); return(0); }
if(ErrorCheck(CHFJPY) > 0)
{ PrintErrorMessage(); return(0); }
if(ErrorCheck(AUDCHF) > 0)
{ PrintErrorMessage(); return(0); }
if(ErrorCheck(USDJPY) > 0)
{ PrintErrorMessage(); return(0); }
if(ErrorCheck(AUDJPY) > 0)
{ PrintErrorMessage(); return(0); }
if(ErrorCheck(AUDUSD) > 0)
{ PrintErrorMessage(); return(0); }
if(ErrorCheck(EURCAD) > 0)
{ PrintErrorMessage(); return(0); }
if(ErrorCheck(GBPCAD) > 0)
{ PrintErrorMessage(); return(0); }
if(ErrorCheck(USDCAD) > 0)
{ PrintErrorMessage(); return(0); }
if(ErrorCheck(CADJPY) > 0)
{ PrintErrorMessage(); return(0); }
if(ErrorCheck(CADCHF) > 0)
{ PrintErrorMessage(); return(0); }
if(ErrorCheck(AUDCAD) > 0)
{ PrintErrorMessage(); return(0); }
DeleteAllObj();

USD = 0; EUR = 0; GBP = 0; CHF = 0;
JPY = 0; AUD = 0; CAD = 0;

double FactorEURUSD = PairDir(EURUSD);
double FactorEURGBP = PairDir(EURGBP);
double FactorEURCHF = PairDir(EURCHF);
double FactorEURJPY = PairDir(EURJPY);
double FactorEURAUD = PairDir(EURAUD);
double FactorGBPUSD = PairDir(GBPUSD);
double FactorGBPCHF = PairDir(GBPCHF);
double FactorGBPJPY = PairDir(GBPJPY);
double FactorGBPAUD = PairDir(GBPAUD);
double FactorUSDCHF = PairDir(USDCHF);
double FactorCHFJPY = PairDir(CHFJPY);
double FactorAUDCHF = PairDir(AUDCHF);
double FactorUSDJPY = PairDir(USDJPY);
double FactorAUDJPY = PairDir(AUDJPY);
double FactorAUDUSD = PairDir(AUDUSD);
double FactorEURCAD = PairDir(EURCAD);
double FactorGBPCAD = PairDir(GBPCAD);
```

```
double FactorUSDCAD = PairDir(USDCAD);
double FactorCADJPY = PairDir(CADJPY);
double FactorCADCHF = PairDir(CADCHF);
double FactorAUDCAD = PairDir(AUDCAD);

if ((FactorEURUSD) > 0)
    { EUR++; USD--; }
else if ((FactorEURUSD) < 0)
    { EUR--; USD++; }

if ((FactorEURGBP) > 0)
    { EUR++; GBP--; }
else if ((FactorEURGBP) < 0)
    { EUR--; GBP++; }

if ((FactorEURCHF) > 0)
    { EUR++; CHF--; }
else if ((FactorEURCHF) < 0)
    { EUR--; CHF++; }

if ((FactorEURJPY) > 0)
    { EUR++; JPY--; }
else if ((FactorEURJPY) < 0)
    { EUR--; JPY++; }

if ((FactorEURAUD) > 0)
    { EUR++; AUD--; }
else if ((FactorEURAUD) < 0)
    { EUR--; AUD++; }

if ((FactorGBPUSD) > 0)
    { GBP++; USD--; }
else if ((FactorGBPUSD) < 0)
    { GBP--; USD++; }

if ((FactorGBPCHF) > 0)
    { GBP++; CHF--; }
else if ((FactorGBPCHF) < 0)
    { GBP--; CHF++; }

if ((FactorGBPJPY) > 0)
    { GBP++; JPY--; }
else if ((FactorGBPJPY) < 0)
    { GBP--; JPY++; }

if ((FactorGBPAUD) > 0)
```

```
    { GBP++; AUD--; }
else if ((FactorGBPAUD) < 0)
    { GBP--; AUD++; }

if ((FactorUSDCHF) > 0)
    { USD++; CHF--; }
else if ((FactorUSDCHF) < 0)
    { USD--; CHF++; }

if ((FactorCHFJPY) > 0)
    { CHF++; JPY--; }
else if ((FactorCHFJPY) < 0)
    { CHF--; JPY++; }

if ((FactorAUDCHF) > 0)
    { AUD++; CHF--; }
else if ((FactorAUDCHF) < 0)
    { AUD--; CHF++; }

if ((FactorUSDJPY) > 0)
    { USD++; JPY--; }
else if ((FactorUSDJPY) < 0)
    { USD--; JPY++; }

if ((FactorAUDJPY) > 0)
    { AUD++; JPY--; }
else if ((FactorAUDJPY) < 0)
    { AUD--; JPY++; }

if ((FactorAUDUSD) > 0)
    { AUD++; USD--; }
else if ((FactorAUDUSD) < 0)
    { AUD--; USD++; }

if ((FactorEURCAD) > 0)
    { EUR++; CAD--; }
else if ((FactorEURCAD) < 0)
    { EUR--; CAD++; }

if ((FactorGBPCAD) > 0)
    { GBP++; CAD--; }
else if ((FactorGBPCAD) < 0)
    { GBP--; CAD++; }

if ((FactorUSDCAD) > 0)
    { USD++; CAD--; }
```

```
   else if ((FactorUSDCAD) < 0)
      { USD--; CAD++; }

   if ((FactorCADJPY) > 0)
      { CAD++; JPY--; }
   else if ((FactorCADJPY) < 0)
      { CAD--; JPY++; }

   if ((FactorCADCHF) > 0)
      { CAD++; CHF--; }
   else if ((FactorCADCHF) < 0)
      { CAD--; CHF++; }

   if ((FactorAUDCAD) > 0)
      { AUD++; CAD--; }
   else if ((FactorAUDCAD) < 0)
      { AUD--; CAD++; }

   if ( USD == 0 && EUR == 0 && JPY == 0 &&
        GBP == 0 && AUD == 0 && CHF == 0 &&
        CAD == 0 )
      TimeLastLoaded = 0;
   else
      TimeLastLoaded = TimeCurrent();

DrawDemand ("EUR" + LabelSign(EUR),   0,   0,
EUR);
DrawDemand ("GBP" + LabelSign(GBP),  50,   0,
GBP);
DrawDemand ("USD" + LabelSign(USD), 100,   0,
USD);
DrawDemand ("JPY" + LabelSign(JPY), 150,   0,
JPY);
DrawDemand ("CHF" + LabelSign(CHF), 200,   0,
CHF);
DrawDemand ("AUD" + LabelSign(AUD), 250,   0,
AUD);
DrawDemand ("CAD" + LabelSign(CAD), 300,   0,
CAD);

   return(0);
   }

string LabelSign (int Factor)
{
   string Label;
```

```
   if (Factor > 0) Label = "+"+Factor;
   else if (Factor < 0) Label = Factor;
   else Label = " "+Factor;
   return (Label);
}

void DrawDemand (string CurrencyName, int
StartX, int StartY, int Qty)
{
DemandLabel (CurrencyName, CurrencyName,
CurrencyName, Gray, StartX + 10, StartY +
41);

if (Qty >= 7)
DemandBlock (CurrencyName, "+7", Lime, StartX
+ 15, StartY +  5);

if (Qty >= 6)
DemandBlock (CurrencyName, "+6", Lime, StartX
+ 15, StartY + 10);

if (Qty >= 5)
DemandBlock (CurrencyName, "+5", Lime, StartX
+ 15, StartY + 15);

if (Qty >= 4)
DemandBlock (CurrencyName, "+4", Lime, StartX
+ 15, StartY + 20);

if (Qty >= 3)
DemandBlock (CurrencyName, "+3", Lime, StartX
+ 15, StartY + 25);

if (Qty >= 2)
DemandBlock (CurrencyName, "+2", Lime, StartX
+ 15, StartY + 30);

if (Qty >= 1)
DemandBlock (CurrencyName, "+1", Lime, StartX
+ 15, StartY + 35);

if (Qty <= -1)
DemandBlock (CurrencyName, "-1",  Red, StartX
+ 15, StartY + 55);

if (Qty <= -2)
```

```
DemandBlock (CurrencyName, "-2",  Red, StartX
+ 15, StartY + 60);

if (Qty <= -3)
DemandBlock (CurrencyName, "-3",  Red, StartX
+ 15, StartY + 65);

if (Qty <= -4)
DemandBlock (CurrencyName, "-4",  Red, StartX
+ 15, StartY + 70);

if (Qty <= -5)
DemandBlock (CurrencyName, "-5",  Red, StartX
+ 15, StartY + 75);

if (Qty <= -6)
DemandBlock (CurrencyName, "-6",  Red, StartX
+ 15, StartY + 80);

if (Qty <= -7)
DemandBlock (CurrencyName, "-7",  Red, StartX
+ 15, StartY + 85);
}


void DemandLabel (string Curr, string
ObjName, string outputText, color
outputColor, int Xoffset, int Yoffset)
{
ObjectCreate("Demand Label " + Curr + " " +
ObjName, OBJ_LABEL, WindowFind(Display_Name),
0, 0, 0);

ObjectSet("Demand Label " + Curr + " " +
ObjName, OBJPROP_XDISTANCE, Xoffset);
ObjectSet("Demand Label " + Curr + " " +
ObjName, OBJPROP_YDISTANCE, Yoffset);

ObjectSetText("Demand Label " + Curr + " " +
ObjName, outputText, 10, "Courier New Bold",
outputColor);
}

void DemandBlock (string Curr, string ObjNum,
color outputColor, int Xoffset, int Yoffset)
{
```

```
ObjectCreate("Demand Block " + Curr + " " +
ObjNum, OBJ_LABEL, WindowFind(Display_Name),
0, 0, 0);
ObjectSet("Demand Block " + Curr + " " +
ObjNum, OBJPROP_XDISTANCE, Xoffset);
ObjectSet("Demand Block " + Curr + " " +
ObjNum, OBJPROP_YDISTANCE, Yoffset);
ObjectSetText("Demand Block " + Curr + " " +
ObjNum, "nnnnnn", 5, "Wingdings",
outputColor);
}

double PairDir (string InputSymbol)
{
   double OutputValue = 0;
   double DataErrorCheck =
     iClose(InputSymbol,PERIOD_D1,1);
   if ( DataErrorCheck == 0 )
   {
      return(0);
   }
   double ADR;
   for(int a=21;a>0;a--)
   {
     ADR += iHigh(InputSymbol,PERIOD_D1,a)
           - iLow(InputSymbol,PERIOD_D1,a);
   }
   ADR = ADR / 21;
   double ReturnA = (
iClose(InputSymbol,TF,1)
   - iClose(InputSymbol,TF,PeriodA) ) / ADR;
   double ReturnB = (
iClose(InputSymbol,TF,1)
   - iClose(InputSymbol,TF,PeriodB) ) / ADR;
   double ReturnC = (
iClose(InputSymbol,TF,1)
   - iClose(InputSymbol,TF,PeriodC) ) / ADR;
   OutputValue = (FactorA * ReturnA) +
    (FactorB * ReturnB) + (FactorC *
ReturnC);
   return(OutputValue);
}

int ErrorCheck (string InputSymbol)
{
   if (iClose(InputSymbol,PERIOD_D1,1) == 0)
```

```
    return(1);
    else return(0);
}

void PrintErrorMessage ()
{
      Comment("LOADING..." +
       "Please check your prefix and
        suffix settings are correct.");
}

void DeleteAllObj ()
{
    int obj_total= ObjectsTotal();
    for (int i= obj_total; i>=0; i--)
    {
       string name= ObjectName(i);
       if (StringSubstr(name,0,6)=="Demand")
       ObjectDelete(name);
    }
}
//End of code for Currency Strength Rank
```

Where is the money moving? That's the question that these tools help to answer for retail traders who don't have access to institutional order flow information.

Being aware of the flow of capital in the interbank FX market is an essential part of preparing a trader for this market. Also remember that certain currencies are heavily tied to specific aspects of the economy. For instance, currencies like the Australian Dollar (AUD) and Canadian Dollar (CAD) are often referred to as "Com Dolls" (Commodity Dollars) because of their correlation to commodities like gold and crude oil. Traditionally, the US Dollar (USD) and the Japanese Yen (JPY) - the currencies of the two largest developed economies of the post-World War II era of the 20th century - are the currencies that gain strength (capital flows into them) during a flight to safety such as a stock market crash. In other words, the US Dollar and Japanese Yen have historically shown strength when there's fear in the global markets.

These "rules" are changing, especially in an environment of so-called currency wars. By using objective tools to measure capital flows, traders won't have to make assumptions based on outside factors. We can see where the money is moving based on simple market data available on every free trading platform.

Tracking which individual currencies are gaining strength (incoming capital flows) and which ones are weakening (outgoing capital flows), by using measures such as Hourly Relative Strength or variations based on data from other time frames, is a far more practical and objective method of tracking the greed and fear phases of the Forex market.

You don't have to choose your currency pairs arbitrarily. With these tools at your disposal, you can decide on which pairs to trade each day based on strength and weakness.

Most importantly, currency pairs with the *strongest in-flow* of capital on the previous day are greater than 55% likely to make a *higher high and a higher low* than the previous day's price action. The currency pair with the *strongest outflows* of capital on the previous day are greater than 55% likely to make a *lower high and lower low*.

While these figures may not sound like much to a beginner, traders quickly learn that they are far more than meets the eye when they learn to use expectancy to ensure profitability in your trading.

CHAPTER 5
ENTRIES, EXITS & EXPECTANCY

Beginners will probably skip straight to this chapter to look for secrets. If that's what you just did, there's nothing to be ashamed of... but you should seriously consider waiting before placing any trades on a live account. Skipping straight to this chapter is a major sign that your attitude about trade entries still has a little maturing to do. If that's the case, you should quickly admit to yourself that you desperately need to reassess your basic understanding of trading as an occupation. You should also realize that if you skipped to this chapter, you just missed one of the rare known long-term edges in this market explained and taught with two custom tools in the previous chapter.

Once you've gauged the times of day when you expect to see a volatility breakout, you already know when the market is likely to blow through established zones of support and resistance. For example, if the EUR/USD has bounced between 1.3050 and 1.3100 throughout the Sydney and Tokyo trading sessions, those price levels (give or take 10 pips or so) are likely to be broken at the Frankfurt open (one hour before London.) Often times, you'll see the first hour of the Frankfurt trading session breakout into a new high or low of the day, but then fail to continue any further in the same direction... until London banks open for business and either take the pair further or reverse the trend altogether. Either way, the move should be bigger. In other words, the first big trend of the day on the majors tends to be backed strongly by the morning of the London banking hours.

After London has taken the major pairs into new trending territory, New York's 8AM will come in approximately five hours later (at most times of year) and the London trend will likely have stalled a little after the UK lunch hour. Within the first two New York banking hours, especially with the American stock market open at 9:30AM in New York's time zone, you'll likely find the beginning of an even stronger trend - which may be a reversal of the London morning trend or sometimes a continuation. Remember, this is the London afternoon occurring at the same time as the New York morning. It's likely to be the time of the biggest trending move of the day, if for no other reason than that two of the world's largest financial centers in Forex are participating in full force at the same time.

Finally, volatility tends to slow down by the New York afternoon and, if it's not a Friday, then the Forex market continues on to the following day's opening hours in Sydney followed by Tokyo - both of which are unlikely to start any major trends far beyond the highs and lows established by London and New York. In other words, expect less volatility and a higher chance of ranging consolidation behavior. Many part-time traders in North America trade the Sydney and Tokyo sessions purely because it lands in the evening and conveniently fits into their schedules if they're still working a full-time job outside of trading. If this is your situation, I'd recommend staying away from trend-following or breakout strategies as the opportunities are few and far in between. Instead, it would make the most sense to focus on mean reversion approaches.

The purpose of this recap of the daily patterns of volatility is to hammer in the idea that no entry method is universal. No entry method works at all times of day. Trying to find one single end-all be-all style of entering and exiting trades is like trying to drive on a highway at one optimal speed during both rush hour as well as other times of day.

Be aware of the times you trade, and be aware of the environment you're trading in.

It should also be worth mentioning that certain times of year tend to be slower. These include the northern hemisphere's summer months - July and August - and the winter holiday month of December. As you might've guessed, this is in large part because of the vacations taken by bank traders in New York and London. The daily patterns of volatility will still hold up during these months (meaning, the first hours of London and New York banking hours will still be more volatile than the Sydney and Tokyo hours of the same day), but the overall volatility of intraday trends would likely be smaller - and at times, there will be little to no major trending moves compared to the more volatile times of year.

Position Sizing and Stop Losses

Before entering, always know your stop loss price, whether you plan to enter it in as an actual order or simply rely on your own discipline to stop out manually. If you're betting on a breakout from a range, it makes sense to plan a stop loss somewhere around the middle of the broken range. If you're entering at the break of a trendline, it makes sense to plan a stop that's fairly tight (a good, clean trendline break tends not to retrace much but you can go for higher probability by placing a stop a little past where price would go if the market retests the trendline.)

Either way, the stop loss should be your guide to position sizing. It makes no sense to trade the same size for an intraday trade with a 30-pip stop and a longer term trade with a 200-pip stop. Every trade should be given roughly the same percentage risk on your account, or at the very least, a properly planned out risk level. (For example, maybe you've got more conviction for trade A than trade B, then you can risk 2% on trade A and only 1% on trade B. Either way, the size of both trades should be based on a planned risk level rather than just some arbitrary trade size.)

This is not a new concept by any means but it's a basic calculation that's worth reviewing and should really be common knowledge for traders at all levels.

Formula for Risk-Adjusted Position Sizing

Standard Lots to trade

=

(Balance) x (% Risked) x (# pips stop) x 0.1

Where "Balance" is your trading account's balance at the time of trade entry; "% Risked" is the percentage of your account that you'll risk on each trade; and, "# pips stop" is the number of pips that your stop loss will be from your entry price. The multiplication by 0.1 is because every Standard Lot (100,000 units) is approximately $10 per pip on USD quoted pairs, so $1 per pip is 0.1 Standard Lot. Multiplying the result by 0.1 gives you the number relative to Standard Lots since most Forex trading platforms designate trade sizes relative to Standard Lots. (You should always check to make sure that this is the case with your broker. Some Mini and Micro accounts have modified the trading platform to show "1.0" as a different trade size.) It's also worth noting that if your account's base currency is not USD, you should be aware of the currency conversion that will take place. Just look up this other currency's current rate against the USD or whichever currency the pair is quoted in. (The quote currency is the one on the right side of the pair's symbol.)

Example: If your account balance is $10,000,

you're planning to risk 2% per trade (2% of $10,000 = $200), and your stop loss is 30 pips from your entry price, then divide $200 by 30, and multiply the result by 0.1 to get the number of Standard Lots you should be trading.

The Scale-In Plan

With all of that out of the way, how do we enter trades?

Well, for manual traders, the first thing you should do is plan how you'll scale into the trade. Don't limit yourself to single-entry, single-exit trading - it only makes it easier for the market (or an unscrupulous retail dealer who is B-Booking you) to hit your stop loss orders. Instead, plan out a zone where you plan to get in - the highest and lowest prices you're willing to enter at - and scale into your planned position only while the market is still within your scale-in zone.

To be clear, please do not take this as an okay to go ahead and average down on losing trades. There's a huge difference between adding to losers and following a professional scale-in plan. If you entered an initial trade at your full trade size, and the price goes against you, there's no excuse for adding to that position then - and if you do, you're not scaling in, you're just giving yourself an excuse while you lose money. Adding to losing trades is one of the most destructive habits that originates from under-developed traders who refuse to acknowledge they can be wrong. Everybody is wrong from time to time. You're human. Accept that, and play on your strengths. Don't let this weakness melt away your account balance.

How is a professional scale-in plan different?

Firstly, when you properly scale into a trade,

you will never enter your full trade size right off the bat. Instead, you plan out your first fraction of your entry, and you know for a fact that you'll be adding to it. And when you do add to this trade, you're also not doing so out of an in-the-moment reaction to the market. You're doing so as part of a planned method of establishing your original full-sized position in multiple steps.

This is an important concept to understand. Never allow yourself to make excuses for your own mistakes. Learn from them, and admit to them, but never try to justify them.

Now, you might ask, "What do you do if the market takes off before you're done scaling in?"

Simple. You have two choices. If you're a relative beginner, just chalk it up to being right and take the smaller profit for now. It's too dangerous to handle any other way at your current stage of development as a trader. (Be honest with yourself about this, it's your own money on the line.)

If you're an experienced trader, meaning you've proven to yourself that you've been able to take controlled losses with discipline for at least two months, then there's another alternative: Quickly add the rest of your position... but immediately tighten up your stops.

If you do this, do not let the market reverse against you - ever. This is important.

You already knew from the start that you

planned to trade a certain size when you're done scaling in. (Preferably, this size should be based on a percentage of risk using your stop loss.) If the market takes off in your favor before you managed to scale into that full size, then there's one thing you already know: The capital in the market is already flowing in your favor. In other words, the near-term trend is on your side.

If this is the case, and you choose to jump in with the remainder of your planned position size, then under no circumstances would it make sense to let this trade go negative, especially relative to that first scale-in price. You're already right; now it's time to find out how right you are. If it turns out you were wrong, then cut your losses small and cut them quickly. There would clearly be another opportunity to enter at a better price, if that first breakout in your favor turns out to be a "fake-out".

In case you haven't pieced it together yet, the technique of scaling into trades is precisely what the vast majority of professional traders who handle large portfolios do as a routine. This is partly by choice, and partly out of necessity. At the sizes traded on a professional trade desk, it's necessary to scale into trades in order to prevent single-handedly causing a large move that could then reverse on you. (Single-handedly creating a negative market environment for the trader.) Putting that aside, it also allows the trader to feel out the market before entering the full trade size. No one is right all the time... but it helps to know how right or how wrong you are.

Plus, if you stagger your stop loss orders a little (which would naturally happen if you scale in with a number of pieces, all with the same relative stop loss distance) you're also making it more difficult for other market participants to hunt your stop losses.

Yes, stop hunting is a real phenomenon - and it's not just a habit of unscrupulous retail dealers, it's also a strategy used by many professional traders at market making banks. One of the easiest weaknesses for a Forex dealer to exploit is the use of a simple single-entry and single-exit style of trading. Don't make yourself unnecessarily vulnerable to your opposition.

Lastly, the overall net effect of each trade should yield a positive expectancy. More on that later.

Sample Entry: Trend Reversal

This is an example of a method of trade entry. Again, if you skipped to this part of the book without building your background knowledge of the rationale behind it (revealed throughout the book before this) you're not psychologically prepared to trade with real money. Plus, you missed some of the keys to actually using this profitably. It's nothing to be ashamed of if you're guilty of that, it's a part of human nature... but I'd recommend reviewing the background information before trading it with real money. By itself, it looks good on cherry-picked examples, but it has no real edge until you learn to apply it at the right times with the right currency pairs.

With that said, I'll introduce a basic entry method - presented in a new context you're unlikely to find in other retail trader education material.

The basic trend reversal is based on an observation of follow-through under certain conditions. This concept is not new by any means, but it's an effective approach that deserves to be reiterated.

On a day with decent trading volume, you'll likely see some form of trend develop in the first few hours of the London session. This may appear as a nice, clean trend that's described by the typical trading educator material as "waves" or "bounces off trendlines." In reality, this trend may even be a parabolic shoot up or down, in a speed that seems analogous to a market panic. Either way, it's a natural part of the market.

Market imbalances come in all shapes and sizes, but they still mean the same thing - there are more orders on one side than the other.

At this point, I should review what exactly an order really is in a financial market because the misconceptions of this concept can be detrimental to your understanding of price trends. Every time you interact with a trade - whether to open it, to close it, or to manage it - you're entering orders. Market orders, limit orders, stop orders, and so on. Orders are the tools used by traders of all sizes and experience to act on the market. So when I mention orders, I'm not only referring to large unmarketable orders (limits) standing at big round numbers. I'm also referring to market orders used by traders to enter or exit quickly. I'm also referring to stop orders that may be one trader's loss-control exit or another trader's method of entry. And, of course, I'm also referring to all sorts of limit orders - including quick flash orders entered by automated "High-Frequency Trading" algorithms.

If and when a market trends, at any time, it's the result of an imbalance in buy orders versus sell orders. If it trends up, then there are more buy orders than sell orders acting on the market. If it trends down, then there are more sell orders than buy orders acting on the market. It's that simple.

What you see on the chart can vary from nice, clean formations that you learned in a technical analysis book to dirty, fast moves that resemble a market crash or short squeeze.

What you're looking for in this example entry method is any of these. It doesn't matter which. Whether it's pretty or ugly, a clear direction is established on a currency pair that showed the most inflows or outflows on the previous trading day, as measured by the tools introduced in previous chapters.

Now, once the dust settles, the phase you're looking for is the first reversal of the day. This often happens when London banks open and reverse the trend of the Sydney and Tokyo sessions. Sometimes, it also happens when New York banks join the action and reverse the trend of the London morning. Either way, just look for the first major reversal.

The classic way to look for this reversal pattern is to draw a trendline. Every trading platform comes with a tool to draw your own trendlines.

First, draw a trendline that connects all of the retracements of the directional move. Preferably at least two clean hits that form a specific angle. (This angle is a universal relation between time and price, especially on lower intraday time frames such as a 15-minute chart.)

Second, use your trading platform's Fibonacci Tool to measure from the point of the trendline break to the peak of the broken trend.

When price breaks through that trend line, you can start to scale in on the opposite side of the now-broken trend.

In other words, if it trended up and broke an upward trendline, scale into a short position. If it trended down and then broke a downward trendline upward, scale into a long position.

You'll have three high probability targets.

Target #1: 61.8% of Peak to Trendline Break. This is shown on the Fibonacci Tool as a 161.8%

extension. This is the highest probability target, but also the level that price will be most likely to hit at high speed immediately following the break of the trendline.

Target #2: 100% of Peak to Trendline Break.

This is also a relatively high probability target, though comparatively lower than Target #1.

These percentages are essentially a measurement of the buying or selling pressure (whichever is opposite the initial trend) that overshoots the first retaliation against the trend. Recall that a trend is only possible if there is an imbalance of orders in the market. (An upward trend is the result of an imbalance with a greater number of buy orders than sell orders acting on the market.) The break of a trendline is a reversal of this imbalance. And when it happens, these Fibonacci percentage levels are the highest probability targets, in no small part because many of the traders on banks' trade desks use them as safety zones to stop accumulating or distributing after a reversal.

What you're doing with the Fibonacci tool in your trading platform is drawing from the point of the trendline break to the peak of the broken trend. Depending on your charting software, it may be necessary to manually add the 200% (2.00) extension level to your Fibonacci tool. 161.8% (1.618) should, however, be included as a standard Fibonacci extension level on most platforms, including MetaTrader.

Notice that if you scaled into a position that averaged somewhere near the initial break of the trendline, give or take a few pips, you could have maintained a very tight stop loss. And not even the most unscrupulous retail broker can justify hitting your stop in this kind of breakout move. So it's safe to say that you'd be fairly safe playing this trade with a broker that's well-regulated by a developed country's government.

If you maintain a risk-reward ratio that is *better than* 1:1, you'd actually need *less than* a 50% win rate to be break even. Of course, this is only an example, and not all styles of trading require this sort of risk-reward, contrary to the claims of typical trader education material. In order to become net profitable, a trader only has to maintain positive expectancy.

Expectancy Formula

Expectancy

$=$

(Win Rate x Win Size)

-

(1 - Win Rate) x (Loss Size)

For example, if your target (Win Size) is 60 pips and your stop loss (Loss Size) is 30 pips, and you make winning trades 50% of the time (Win Rate), you'll have positive expectancy. In fact, with an average win size twice as large as your average loss size, you only need a 34% Win Rate to breakeven. Anything higher will produce a profit of some amount.

Of course, making money with a win rate of 35% to 50% is incredibly difficult for traders in the real world, both psychologically and in some case, practically if it requires a very strict ability to catch every single opportunity that the method is assumed to take. It's also not entirely practical in many real-world cases to target a win size twice the size of a stop loss simply because real-world markets don't move in straight lines.

The reality that many trading educators fail to

mention is that when it comes to strategies that yield incredibly high win rates (which, of course, are relatively rare) really do not require a favorable risk-reward ratio to succeed. In fact, if you experiment with the Expectancy formula above, you'll find that a strategy that achieves greater than 50% win rate can easily be traded with 1:1 risk-reward (or worse, as the win rate increases.)

This is, of course, the sort of information that beginners are rarely taught simply because the vast majority of trading methods will never yield such a high win rate. Remember, there needs to be a rational and objective reason to be confident that such a win rate can and will be sustained well into the future before deciding to trade using unfavorable risk-reward ratios.

Recall now that the previous chapters introduced a way to find a greater than 55% probability of a new high or new low being established under specific conditions. Armed with that information, you will be able to place intraday trades knowing the likely targets that will be hit, and the areas unlikely to be hit.

Realistically, you should simply be aiming to achieve positive expectancy, and to keep your risk scaled to a conservative percentage of your account. Whether the edge presented in this book will remain effective into the future or not, you should learn and internalize this principle of expectancy and always assess your new ideas and trade plans accordingly.

You may also be wondering why this discussion of expectancy lands in the entries and exits chapter of this book rather than a separate Money Management chapter as in many other books on trading. The main reason I decided to do it this way is to emphasize that expectancy is a consideration for the trader at the stage of trade planning. It should never be put off as an issue to worry about another time, which beginners often do with "Money Management" issues. Rather, it's a core factor to address before even considering the validity of a particular entry and exit strategy for any trading method.

The most important lesson here is not any one, single method of entering and exiting trades, or even the method of determining targets. The lesson is that this is the sort of entry you should be hunting for - strategies with positive expectancy. Any time you find an edge that achieves a larger, positive expectancy figure, the added gains will just be icing on your profitability cake. Pounce on those opportunities for as long as they might last.

CHAPTER 6
TRADE MANAGEMENT

Once you're in a trade, you should be aware of the potential forces that are the most likely to halt your most favorable market movements in their tracks... and factors that might even turn the winning trade against you. Most of all, you need to be aware of your interpretation of what's happening.

Order flow information is a major asset for a day trader. Of course, for retail traders in the Forex market, reliable order data is incredibly hard to come by. Aside from accepting your limitations, you should also tackle them in the best ways you can. Measuring capital flows using the tools provided in this book are among the strategies you can use to tackle this problem.

Another method is a simple awareness of potential reversal price zones.

The most commonly-known reversal zones where price could potentially stall are Support and Resistance, and Round Numbers. These concepts have been beat to death in many education programs and internet resources, but I'll quickly review them in case you've picked up any misinformation along the way.

Support and Resistance refer to the same thing, only that Support is a zone below the current price and Resistance is a zone above. In reality, it doesn't make much of a difference if you flipped the chart upside down - they still do the same thing.

Here are straight definitions that you're unlikely

to have been taught accurately by the majority of retail Forex trader resources:

Support and Resistance zones are areas of price - typically 5 to 10 pips in size on majors - where historical price action has reversed, and therefore holds a greater than 50% probability of reversing again in the future.

Notice, first of all, that I did not refer to them as specific price levels. They aren't. They're small zones where price might stall for a bit, and potentially (with greater than 50% probability) reverse as observed in the past.

Secondly, I emphasize that their significance is only that they provide greater than 50% certainty. You can choose any arbitrary price on the chart, and there's a 50% certainty that future price action could reverse there. That's the nature of the market... from the point of view of a trader who has no further detailed information. Support and Resistance zones, however, are by definition areas that already acted in the past as reversal areas. There's no concrete guarantee that the large, institutional limit orders that succeeded in protecting these zones in the past will still be there the next time price reaches it... but there's a greater than 50% probability that it might.

That's all you really know, based on Support and Resistance zones. Beyond that, you're making assumptions based on other sources of information (or based on no real objective data, which isn't a great habit to build.)

The other well-known zones of potential reversals are the big round numbers. Double-zero figures like 1.3400 on EUR/USD or 84.00 on USD/JPY. (Recall: Regardless of sub-pips and other pricing granularities, the pip value on anything *other than* a JPY-quoted pair is the fourth decimal place. On JPY-quoted pairs, it's the second. This is a basic concept that you should already be familiar with before placing a live trade, but it's worth clearing up any confusion in terminology when discussing round numbers.) Smaller round numbers include 20, 50, and 80. (For example, 1.3620 on EUR/USD or 94.50 on USD/JPY.)

Like historical Support and Resistance zones, these are also price zones where large institutional limit orders may or may not protect the zone in the future. The only real use to a trader is that they tend to protect these zones with greater than 50% probability. (And, yes, many historical Support and Resistance zones are, in fact, on one of these round numbers. This is in no small part because Corporates and Sovereigns tend not to care for the intricacies of intraday price action on the Forex market, and would place orders on large round numbers. Other factors include the fact that large traders on the banks' Forex dealing desks tend to be aware of this phenomenon and take advantage of it for the same reasons you would.)

Also, aside from the potential of large institutional limit orders standing in the way of a trend, another type of price level to be aware of are nearby options strike prices when they're soon to expire. Consult with the Chicago Board Options Exchange (CBOE) official web site and material to find information on their FX options nearing their expiration dates. These price levels are guarded by large market participants with more determination than almost any other type of price level in most cases. Be aware of them, and use them to your advantage.

Now, after all this talk of potential reversal zones, it's worth recalling why this is all in a chapter about trade management. And that's because you should be aware of the areas where price might stall.

Beginners tend to place far too much emphasis on trade entries, and not enough on trade management - especially when a trade goes into profit. If you immediately close the trade in profit every time it goes green, you're guaranteed to net out to a horrible risk-reward ratio unless you take losses the same way (and most beginners would never think to do that!)

The best way to train yourself out of this fear of losing profits (even when they're tiny) is to become intimately familiar with the price zones where the market is actually likely to stop and reverse. None of these are guaranteed, but they're more likely - and much better for your risk-reward ratio - than that price you might have closed the trade for at only one or two pips in the green.

CHAPTER 7
A NEW LOOK AT TRADER PSYCHOLOGY

In 1970, Walter Mischel and Ebbe B. Ebbesen conducted an experiment on delayed gratification that's come to be known as the Marshmallow Experiment. Children were given an immediate reward (a marshmallow or other treat) and were then told to wait. If the child succeeded in waiting, rather than eating the immediate reward, they were given a second reward. In the follow-up studies on the participants of this experiment, Mischel found that the children who were able to delay gratification (able to wait for a greater total reward rather than indulging in the first reward immediately) also scored higher on their SAT's.

The majority of successful traders exhibit similar abilities to those who performed well in the Marshmallow Experiment. Despite being surrounded by the same instant-gratification culture, and sometimes in spite of unreliable promises from parents and peers, successful traders continue to outperform the majority in terms of the ability to delay gratification.

Does any of this mean you have to be a natural at this ability? Not at all.

For the vast majority of people, the ability to delay gratification can be learned. In fact, for most of you who may not have naturally had this ability, you've already been trained with some degree of the ability by the end of high school. It's a natural expectation of you, in the process of maturing.

As a trader, however, you'll quickly find that the ability to delay gratification can be incredibly difficult to attain. Beginners often close out a trade as soon as it comes into a miniscule extent of profit. The vast majority of beginners also tend to come up with excuse after excuse to hold onto losing trades. Even so-called professionals have been found guilty of this psychological trap - including a hedge fund called Long-Term Capital Management that came dangerously close to taking the entire global financial system down with them in the process.

The ability to cut losses quickly and wait for profits to grow is the most obvious benefit of the ability to delay gratification. The immediate reward of seeing a trade close in the green must be delayed, while the fear of taking a loss must be accepted.

In a longer term horizon, the ability also comes in handy for the development of your trading prowess. There's no reason to jump straight into the deep end; yet, so many beginner traders try to trade beyond their means from day one.

If your total risk capital is $100 today, then trade as if it's $100. Don't over-leverage yourself, hoping to multiply that capital by unrealistic amounts overnight. Be patient. If you trade with favorable risk-reward ratios, and employ high probability trading strategies, there's no reason to risk losing your entire account on every trade.

Of course, the natural human tendency is to gravitate toward apparent opportunities for instant gratification, even if you've been trained to know deep down that it can't work that way. When retail brokers offer upwards of 400:1 leverage, it's easy to see why a large percentage of individual Forex traders quickly wipe out their account balances.

The reality is that the Forex market isn't all that different from other financial markets such as equities (stocks), futures, or fixed income. It never has been, when it comes down to the mechanics of the actual price action. The biggest driving factor behind the enormous losses racked up by early generations of retail Forex traders was the ridiculously high leverage.

If a hedge fund made up of the best and brightest of America's Ivy league "Quants" can't survive over-leveraging and letting losses run... what chance does a beginner trader, with no statistically-backed strategy, really have in the long run?

The first step to turning this pattern around is to learn that the long-term reward does, in fact, equate to something far greater than those one or two pips you locked in by luck as a beginner. It's even better than trying to double your account overnight - simply because it's actually sustainable, and doubling accounts on a daily basis is not.

Drill this into your head. Internalize it. If you consistently make a good (and realistic) percentage of gain on your account, month after month, you will end up far more wealthy than you are today. If you try to "cheat" the system, and double or triple your account in anything less than two years, you'll end up poorer than you are today.

A zero account balance doesn't help anyone. In fact, this applies to unscrupulous Forex brokers as well: A quick gain against a B-Book account brought to zero might seem great today, but you're only driving a potential long-term customer onto the road toward giving up forever. Small commissions and spread mark-ups on A-Book accounts over time will trump a few small wiped-out B-Book accounts.

From either point of view, your goal should be to play for the long haul. Immediate gratification is overrated.

As a trader, you should also be aware that the trader's psychology is indeed as much of an issue for designers of automated trading systems as it is for manual traders. If the designer of an automated algorithm inappropriately reacts to every loss - even losses that were statistically predictable and within acceptable risk parameters during the design phase - and the trader (or system programmer) panics then stops or switch systems prematurely, opportunities for long term profits will be lost.

For manual traders, this is a far more obvious issue from a day-to-day viewpoint, especially when professional traders have learnt to adapt and trade flexibly and act appropriately to prevailing market conditions. This adaptive ability inherently runs the risk of causing the trader to second guess every trade. Not to mention that beginners are, in general, more likely to overreact emotionally to losing trades.

Always react to losses the way a normal functioning adult should to bad weather. It's not ideal but it's not within your control either - and it just comes with the package. Don't dwell on it; move on. In fact, other aspects of your life would likely be improved with a similar attitude.

Another common cause of frustration to beginners is that the market constantly appears to do the opposite of what you believed it "should" have done.

Let go of your preconceived opinions of where you think the market "should" go. Whatever personal connections or gripes you may have with the countries of the currencies you trade - forget about them. Are you convinced that the country of the pair's quote currency is headed to a collapse? Forget about it during short-term trading. Are you convinced that the country of the pair's base currency will raise interest rates next month? Fine. Go adjust your long term positions accordingly... but forget about it during the intraday session. Even if economic news hits and confirms a positive for the currency, there's a good chance it'll fall like a rock - not the least of the reasons being that the market tends to price these things in long before the actual news release.

The movements during each trading session can trend in the completely opposite direction from where you think it "should" end up, no matter how right or wrong you may be about the future. In fact, even if your belief is entirely correct, the currency can still trend strongly in the opposite direction for factors you hadn't considered. If you let this prevent you from trading with discipline, you're not thinking like a professional trader.

Be objective. Leave your preconceived ideas and opinions about the future of the currency for your next dinner party or internet social network comment. Keep your head clear of these biases, these distractions, when you're trading with short term market movements.

Finally, there's the psychological attitude toward winning strategies.

There's a common misconception among beginner traders that any old strategy can somehow be magically transformed into a consistently profitable money-making machine... if only you had the discipline to maintain an inhumanly perfect psychological reaction to every trade.

This is simply not true, and is about as logical as asserting that if you keep jumping up and down on a concrete road, then if - and only if - you can psychological accept failure a billion times without flinching, you will magically break straight through the ground and end up in New Zealand eventually. (Or, if you happen to actually live in New Zealand, you can replace that with New York City.)

The fact is that the trading strategy itself is

equally, if not more, important than trader psychology. A poor handle on trader psychology will simply stand in the way.

The original well-meaning root behind many of these dogmatic belief systems about trading psychology began with the problem that beginners naturally placed far too much emphasis on entries and exits, and too little on controlling their own psychology. Naturally, from that starting point, a major overhaul of the trader's psychology would most definitely improve his or her performance. There's no doubt about that. The problem arises when traders and online educators misunderstand the original message, and suddenly it's psychology and money management that becomes the end-all and be-all solution to every possible problem with a trader's profitability.

Be realistic. That's simply not possible.

Live in the real world... because that's where your account balance has to live. If your personality requires the occasional push from some form of meditation or deep philosophical reflection, go right ahead... while the Forex market's closed for the weekend. When it comes time to make decisions that will affect your bottom line, turn your left brain on and see the difference between what does and doesn't objectively make sense. The key to profitability is a method that produces a high enough risk-reward ratio for your win rate, or a high enough win rate for your risk-reward ratio. That's all there is to it. The rest is about avoiding the pitfalls of standing in your own way by making irrational decisions such as cutting winning trades short or letting losses run.

You're in a highly competitive business. Accept responsibility for your choices, and don't volunteer to be the easy prey.

CHAPTER 8
STATISTICAL TRADING BASICS

No strategy is likely to remain profitable forever. A vital skill for a professional trader is the ability to develop your own trading strategies. Having the ability to test your ideas with quantifiable data helps a trader's confidence while providing a logical reason to choose one idea over another.

This chapter is an introduction to this facet of the business of trading. It will be a basic introduction to the development of strategies under the same basic premises that are used by many institutional market participants - adapted for everyone who isn't already a professional quantitative trader and programmer.

The purpose of this chapter is not to hand you a cut-and-dry strategy. Instead, the purpose of this chapter is to teach you the basics of developing your own strategies based on robust principles that will allow you to find not only today's profitable strategies but also tomorrow's and next year's. By following the simple exercises in this chapter, you should be able to build a core understanding of how to research basic ideas in a statistically-backed method using simple and free software packages.

The software of choice in the step-by-step instructions are MetaTrader 4 (a free trading platform offered by the majority of FX brokers even without a live account as free demo accounts give you access to it) and OpenOffice Calc (an open source spreadsheet application, essentially a free cross-platform clone of Microsoft Excel.) MetaTrader 4 lacks many of the strengths of other trading platforms and OpenOffice Calc lacks the VBA scripting features of Excel (as of this writing) but for the purposes of this introduction, they should suffice and, most importantly for struggling traders on a budget, they both cost absolutely nothing to begin to use for this purpose.

Once you've learned the basics through this tutorial, you should be able to expand on the concepts using other tools to perform more complex equivalents to this exercise. For now, you'll be pleasantly surprised how much can be achieved with these basic tools alone.

Step 1: The Strategy Idea

Suppose you thought of a simple theory about the behavior of price in the Forex market. For the purposes of this exercise, your hypothetical theory is that you suspect if a currency pair opens and closes a one-hour period (a single candle or OHLC bar on a chart that is set to a one-hour period) within the top half of the same hour's entire range, it's more likely that the following hour will not make a new low.

To be clear, that's "and" - meaning both the open price of the hour *and* the close price of the hour are within the top 50% of the same hour's full range. If, and only if, that criteria is met, you suspect then that the following hour will more likely than not fail to make a new low (the next hour's low will exceed this hour's low.)

Likewise, you suspect that if both the open and the close of the current hour are below the middle of this hour's range, then the next hour is more likely to fail to make a new high (lower high than the current hour's high.)

At a very basic level, this theory of yours closely resembles the core logic of many "price action patterns" as hammers, pin bars, and other reversal patterns commonly traded by price action traders. The concept used in this example is slightly simplified so that we can test it using nothing but plain text historical data in a free spreadsheet application.

Step 2: The Testing Method

The testing method for your theory will be simple. We will take a sample of historical price data for an arbitrary range of time. This data consists of the open, high, low, and close prices for each hour within the range.

We will then use the spreadsheet to calculate the half way point of each hour's range (high minus low, divided by two, added to the low price.) And then we test to see if each hour's open and close prices are both (not either/or but both) higher than that half way point; as well as whether both open and close prices are lower than that half way point. Remember, the typical hour will not have both the open as well as the close on the same half (above nor below the half way point) of the full range of the hour so this step will identify the relatively unusual characteristic of an hour that shows a particular bias in either buying or selling pressure. If both open and close of an hour is above the half way point, we will mark it as bullish for the next hour. Likewise, if both open and close of an hour is below the half way point, we will mark it as bearish for the next hour.

Lastly, we'll test whether or not the hour that follows a "bullish" signal actually fails to break the low of the previous hour; and whether or not the hour that follows a "bearish" signal fails to break the high of the previous hour.

Step 3: Install the Free Software

If you do not already have a version of MetaTrader 4 installed on your computer, or if you prefer a fresh installation even if you already do, go ahead and download a fresh copy from any broker that offers MT4. Simply open a free demo account from any broker that offers accounts to traders in your country and run the platform.

Next, install the free Calc spreadsheet application from OpenOffice.org -- this is a free open source software package that's compatible with Windows, Linux, and Mac OS. (Of course, MetaTrader is a native Windows application, but a number of free emulation software packages are available for other operating systems that should allow you to run MetaTrader as well.)

Step 4: Load Market Data into a Spreadsheet

For this exercise, we're going to use historical data provided for free by the MetaQuotes' (the developers of MetaTrader) history servers. While the historical data provided by MetaQuotes is anything but perfect, it should suffice for the purposes of this exercise. (In the future, if you're interested in cleaner historical data in lower time frames for long periods into the past, there are a number of other sources including free tick data from the Swiss ECN broker, Dukascopy, as well as Gain Capital, and others. If you're interested in commercial data, there's also a wide selection with variable quality data, but that's beyond the scope of this book.)

To download a set of historical hourly open, high, low, and close prices for this exercise, we'll use MetaTrader's built-in History Center.

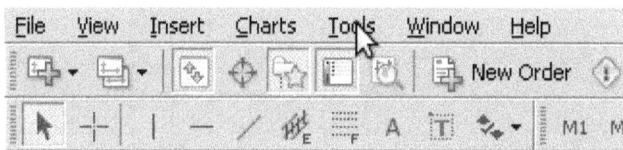

First, run your installation of the MetaTrader software and then go to the Tools menu and choose "History Center".

Once the History Center window appears, click

on a currency pair on the left to expand it, then double-click the "1 Hour (H1)" timeframe.

This will load a small set of one-hour bars, if any, that may already be loaded on your copy of MetaTrader. Next, press the "Download" button at the bottom-left corner of the History Center window to download more rows of data from the MetaTrader history server.

As a side note, if you're interested in loading a larger set of data for this step, you can increase the maximum amount of historical data loaded by MetaTrader by going to Tools, Options, Charts, and increasing the number in "Max bars in history" and "Max bars in chart". However, this is not necessary for this exercise as we are just using a small subset of hourly bars for the purposes of a simple spreadsheet test.

When the software finishes downloading a new

set of hourly data from the server, click on the "Export" button and choose a folder to save the resulting CSV (Comma Separated Variables) file to. (This file format is also compatible with other software packages and applications including Excel and even PHP and MySQL web applications, but for the purposes of this exercise, we'll stick with the Calc spreadsheet.) You may choose any folder on your hard drive -- even the Desktop if that's convenient for you.

After the CSV file is saved in a folder on your hard drive, open it using the OpenOffice Calc spreadsheet application.

File Edit View Insert Format Tools Data Window Help

Arial   10

A1 $f(x)$ Σ = 1999.10.01

	A	B	C	D	E	F	G
1	1999.10.01	00:00	1.0679	1.0684	1.0637	1.0638	75
2	1999.10.01	01:00	1.0637	1.0673	1.0636	1.067	42
3	1999.10.01	02:00	1.0669	1.0684	1.0669	1.0679	84
4	1999.10.01	03:00	1.0681	1.0685	1.0672	1.0683	94
5	1999.10.01	04:00	1.0683	1.0716	1.0682	1.0714	129
6	1999.10.01	05:00	1.0714	1.0723	1.0708	1.0718	122
7	1999.10.01	06:00	1.0718	1.0721	1.0709	1.0712	150

It should appear as a spreadsheet with dates in the first column, times in the second column (which should be one hour apart since you chose the one-hour timeframe in the MetaTrader History Center), followed by Open, High, Low, Close, and Tick Volume figures for each row (hour) respectively.

If you've had any experience with using historical data from other markets in a spreadsheet, you might notice two differences. Firstly, unlike stock data, there is no "Adjusted Close" price. This is because Adjusted Close is a method of compensating for stock splits and reverse splits, dividend payments, and other factors that affect the true return of a stock. None of these factors apply to currency pairs on a universal level. Secondly, the volume column is more accurately referred to as tick volume because, due to the decentralized nature of the FX markets, there is no central reporting system for all transactions and therefore we cannot attain truly accurate trade volumes. (Tick volumes are a close approximation but they mostly tell us the number of changes in the bid and ask prices rather than actual transactions.) We will not use volumes in any way in this exercise, but it's worth remembering this limitation of all sources of historical FX data in case you decide to use it for other purposes in the future.

Step 5: Learn Spreadsheet Calculations

To start with our calculations in the spreadsheet, we'll deal first with only the top row. If you're already proficient in Calc or even Excel, this process should already be familiar to you. Either way, this exercise will continue to guide you through the process step-by-step. Don't worry about any of the rows below the very top row just yet; we'll deal with them afterward using a very basic yet mostly-automated technique that's universal to spreadsheet applications.

Before we begin typing into the spreadsheet, understand that the next steps we are performing will create cells on the spreadsheet in new columns (to the right of the historical data loaded from the CSV file) which will later be copied and pasted down to other rows to do the same calculations. Each column will essentially be each of the testing and calculation steps mentioned in Step 2.

The first of these calculations is a formula that finds the half way point of each hour: "Low + (0.5 x (High - Low))".

To translate this formula into one that can be understood by a spreadsheet, we will type the following into cell "H1":

```
=E1+(0.5*(D1-E1))
```

Then press enter. (Make sure you type it exactly as shown, including the leading "equals" sign. This formula format will work in Calc as well as Excel.)

Note that D1 refers to the High on the first row and E1 refers to the Low. As long as you didn't add or remove any columns from the spreadsheet after loading the CSV file, these column letters should remain consistent with your own copy of this file.

	E	F	G	H
	1.0637	1.0638	75	1.06605
	1.0636	1.067	42	

=E1+(0.5*(D1-E1))

Next, we will move to the next column (column letter "I") and type into the cell on the first row, "I1" our formula for determining whether this hour is a bullish signal.

Recall that our criteria for a bullish signal was a test for whether or not both the open price as well as the close price of this hour (this row) are above the half way point, which we just calculated in column "H". In column "I" then, it should output a "1" if it is, in fact, a bullish signal. If not, then it will output a "0". (You may choose other outputs, but 1 and 0 allow for fast "if" statements in later columns, so we'll stick with them in this exercise. Just remember that we are using 1 for "yes" and 0 for "no".)

To do this, type the following formula into the cell "I1":

```
=IF(AND(C1>H1,F1>H1),1,0)
```

To review some spreadsheet formula basics, this is an "AND" statement nested inside of an "IF" statement. It's telling the spreadsheet application, "IF the open price is greater than the halfway point AND the close price is greater than the halfway point, then output a number 1 in this cell, else output a number 0 in this cell."

```
=IF(AND(C1>H1,F1>H1),1,0)
```

E	F	G	H	I
1.0637	1.0638	75	1.06605	0
1.0636	1.067	42		

In the next column, "J", we'll do the same, except we will be testing for a bearish signal rather than a bullish one. (We'll be testing for whether both the open and close are below, rather than above, the half way point.)

In cell "J1", enter the following formula:

```
=IF(AND(C1<H1,F1<H1),1,0)
```

To reiterate this formula in plain English, we are telling the spreadsheet application, "IF the open price is less than the halfway point AND the close price is less than the halfway point, then output a number 1 in this cell, else output a number 0 in this cell." (Notice that this formula tests for "less than" for the bearish signal instead of "greater than" as with the bullish signal.)

=IF(AND(C1<H1,F1<H1),1,0)						
E	F	G	H	I	J	
1.0637	1.0638	75	1.06605		0	0
1.0636	1.067	42				

Next, let's copy the top row of the columns we just worked on and paste them down to the bottom of the sheet. Spreadsheets understand the relativity of cells to the one referring to them in a formula, so there's no need to change any of them manually. Simply copy the top row and once you paste them below, they'll automatically refer to the respective row they reside on.

The fastest way to do this is to select the cells you just added ("H1", "I1", and "J1") then click on the bottom-right corner of the selection and drag your mouse downward to the bottom of the spreadsheet.

I	J
0	0
0	0
0	0
1	0
0	0
0	0
0	0
0	0
0	0
0	0
0	0

This is a trick that does the same as selecting a number of cells and using "Copy" followed by selecting the target cells and using "Paste" but you can do it either way you prefer.

You now have the first columns that calculate bullish and bearish signals for every row of historical data that you had loaded earlier from the MetaTrader History Center.

Next, we will create a column that finds whether or not the following hour (not the hour itself) fits a criteria based on whether the preceding hour returned a bullish or bearish signal. Due to the fact that these columns will have to rely on the previous row's data in order to determine a true or false reading, we will have to start these columns on the 2nd row.

On the second row of column "K" (cell "K2"),

enter the following formula:

```
=IF(AND(I1=1,E2>E1),1,0)
```

In plain English, this formula tells the Spreadsheet application, "IF the previous hour was indeed a bullish signal (bull signal column returned 1 on previous row) AND the low of the current hour is greater than the low of the previous hour, then output a number 1 in this cell, else output a number 0 in this cell."

=IF(AND(I1=1,E2>E1),1,0)			
H	I	J	K
1.06605	0	0	
1.06545	0	0	0
1.06765	0	0	

In the 2nd row of the following column, we repeat this process. Type the following into cell "L2":

```
=IF(AND(J1=1,D2<D1),1,0)
```

This formula in plain English reads, "IF the previous hour was indeed a bearish signal (bear signal column returned 1 on previous row) AND the high of the current hour is less than the high of the previous hour, then output a number 1 in this cell, else output a number 0 in this cell."

	=IF(AND(J1=1,D2<D1),1,0)

	I	J	K	L
)5	0	0		
45	0	0	0	0
₅₅	0	0		

Now, we repeat the copy and paste process by highlighting cells "K1" and "L1" then clicking on the bottom right corner of the selection and dragging it down to the bottom of the spreadsheet.

	I	J	K	L
)5	0	0		
45	0	0	0	0
35	0	0	0	0
35	1	0	0	0
39	0	0	1	0
55	0	0	0	0

We now have two columns that check whether or not, if a bullish signal was found on the previous hour the current hour's low did not break the previous hour's low; and if a bearish signal was found on the previous hour the current hour's high did not break the previous hour's high.

Finally, we can calculate the percentages in order to test the theory proposed in Step 1.

In cell "M2", write, "Bullish Low Held". (This, of course, is for your own visual reference and is not necessary for the spreadsheet to do its job.)

Then, enter the following formula in cell "N2":

```
=SUM(K1:K99999)/SUM(I1:I99999)
```

Or, if you are using a recent version of Microsoft Excel, this formula can be shortened as:

```
=SUM(K:K)/SUM(I:I)
```

This means the same thing, but recent versions of Excel would understand the sum of "K:K" to mean the sum of every value within column "K" and likewise for column "I".

As you might've guessed by now, this formula is telling the spreadsheet application, "add all of the values of column K together and divide that by values of column I all added together." (Recall that for every yes, we outputted a number 1 and for every no, we outputted a number 0. This made it much easier for us to calculate the total number of "yes" responses on each column by simply taking the sum of the entire column.)

	L	M	N	
=SUM(K1:K99999)/SUM(I1:I99999)				
0	0	Bullish Low Held	61.69%	
0	0			
0	0			

The result will be a decimal number. To clean it up, right-click on cell "N2" and choose "Format Cell". Choose "Number" then "Percentage". This will convert the decimal value into a more conveniently readable percentage figure.

Finally, write, "Bearish High Held" in cell "M3" for human reference, then enter the following formula into cell "N3":

```
=SUM(L1:L99999)/SUM(J1:J99999)
```

Again, using recent versions of Excel, you can alternatively use the shortened version:

```
=SUM(L:L)/SUM(J:J)
```

It should be self-explanatory at this point that you are, again, telling the spreadsheet to divide a column's total by another column's total. This time, of course, you are dealing with columns "L" and "J".

=SUM(L1:L99999)/SUM(J1:J99999)		
L	M	N
0	0 Bullish Low Held	61.69%
0	0 Bearish High Held	61.13%
0	0	

Again, right click on "N2" and choose "Format

Cell", then "Number" and lastly "Percentage", to make it a nicely readable percentage figure.

Note that the Calc versions of the formulas in "N2" and "N3" are assuming that you loaded less than 99,999 hours of data. If you're dealing with more data than this figure, feel free to increase the "99999" parts of the sum formula in both cells to a larger number.

You're done!

In the example data we used for the AUD/USD pair, the percentages were above 60% on both cells which gives us a higher than 10% edge above 50/50 if we had traded using this statistic. By the time you test this using recent data, the percentages may be different, but you should have gained a basic idea of how to begin researching similar concepts using basic and freely available tools.

Remember that the purpose of this exercise is for you to learn how to test a theory like this using raw historical data and a spreadsheet. Whether the theory turns out to be true or not is not the point because the majority of your own theories will likely turn out to be false. And you will simply move on to the next theory until you find your next core strategy. That new strategy may become your bread and butter for decades to come. Or it may just be something you add to your toolbox for a short time. Either way, you will still continue to test new theories, knowing that you'll need to get used to that habit. In fact, it'll be one of your greatest strengths as a trader when you develop the ability to do this continuously with new ideas.

Markets change. Now you can adapt.

Your Future in Automated Trading

Where can you go from here?

Not everyone is cut out for automated trading. Some people are more naturally inclined toward this side of the business than others. That's perfectly fine. At the very least, even if you're a manual trading purist, it should be worth investigating this end of your line of work if for nothing more than to expand your knowledge of what you're up against. Namely, automated systems designed by other traders.

If you are inclined to dive deeper into the automated end of the pool, you should first learn other variations of spreadsheet formula tricks to test for other ideas. If you haven't already, consider learning a few programming languages to adapt this spreadsheet into a higher performance application. Maybe create a web application using PHP and MySQL.

Aside from trading, an excellent use of your time would be to put aside any natural fears and learn various forms of coding even if you have little to no background in the computer programming field. Gaining intimate familiarity with databases like MySQL and programming languages ranging from Java and C++ to Visual Basic for Applications (VBA) and, arguably, even MetaTrader MQL4 as a starting point, would be infinitely advantageous for traders in the 21st century. If the very idea of learning about any of it intimidates you at first, start with an Excel spreadsheet. After all, the majority of trading floors on Wall Street are lined with computers running Excel to this day. Depending on the complexity of your strategy, it's often possible to test or even execute many of your strategies using Excel formulas combined with its built-in Visual Basic for Applications (VBA) language.

Depending on how you typically tend to learn new concepts the most effectively, you could either take the time to sign up for a basic class in programming with one of these languages. Or if you're naturally an independent learner - which, over time, I had come to learn that I always had been - you may be able to train yourself in many of these programming languages by simply getting the basics down via tutorials, and then simply using Google (or any other favorite search engine of yours... in case the world's changed significantly after the time of this writing) to lookup the specifics on whatever it is you need to accomplish in your strategy or backtest.

For example, if you've decided to start your journey with the MetaTrader language, then once you've got the basics of MQL4 down from a couple of MetaQuotes' basic tutorial documents, you can begin putting your knowledge to use by downloading one of the thousands of free pieces of MQL4 source code available all over the internet and you can then modify it to achieve something you might have an idea for. For instance, if a particular piece of the code has you stumped, just search for it on Google. (For example, to refer to the high of the previous hour, just enter into a search engine, "MQL4 high". Odds are, the full explanation of the built-in "iHigh" function in MQL4 will show up among the top search results.)

The idea of delving into programming might be incredibly alien to many traders, depending on your knowledge background in the area and the trends within the finance industry in recent years. Even if you were once dead set on never touching it with a ten foot pole, I'd suggest that it's worth keeping the possibility in your head for when the time comes. Any way to give you an alternate method to tackle the markets will only help you become a more well-rounded trader somewhere down the road. It also doesn't hurt to consider that many Wall Street trading floors have, in recent years, progressively evolved from a place full of former college athletes and alpha jocks to quantitative traders who better resemble programming nerds. It's always worth learning about other participants' approaches in order to gain a more accurate idea of what you're going to be up against in today's trading environment. After all, the same attitude about other aspects of trading will definitely move your career forward in this business.

The possibilities are endless... but without a basic foundation, many traders never even consider taking a step onto this road at all. So I hope this exercise has succeeded in helping to nudge you in the right direction to investigate further.

CHAPTER 9
PERSONAL GROWTH AS A TRADER

Trade. It's the only proven way to gain the kind of market experience that leads to actually improving in your performance. You've learned the core information. Now, practice putting yourself in the trenches of the market as often as possible.

It's far too easy to accept the advice to, "work hard at it." In this case, you need to do the *right kind of* hard work.

Struggling traders tend to waste hours on online message boards, either hopping from system to system or arguing for their own dogmatic beliefs on topics they're far from experts in. In the age of social networks, I realize the inherent difficulty in efforts to avoid wasting time on social networking sites. But for struggling traders, this often translates into hours and hours of time wasted on trading related forums and communities. In moderation, this is perfectly fine especially if you're able to connect with other like-minded individuals. It becomes a problem when more of your time is spent jumping from system to system developed by people who have never had a single net profitable year under their belt. Instead, the same amount of time and effort could have been far better directed toward gaining actual market experience through real world trading.

Interest and enthusiasm in the markets, and in the history and inner workings of FX itself, is perfectly fine. Just commit yourself to directing more of that interest and enthusiasm toward watching the market - how it moves, how it reacts to events, how and when it speeds up or slows down at specific price areas. This is a 24/5 market, there's rarely a time of day that you can't observe some specific form of price action that will help you develop a better intuitive understanding of the market as a whole.

One of the most common analogies for traders is the comparison of trading to playing a professional sport. In many respects, it makes sense that this is the go-to analogy. Of course, to gain the upper hand in this highly competitive dog eat dog business, you should always be on the lookout for alternate points of view that the majority may not have already thought of or may not be comfortable with. For instance, rather than comparing your performance to a professional athlete's psychology, how about the mindset of a stripper? Consider that the crowd you're reading is a predominantly male group whose composure and rational risk management would be easily threatened by the idea of the possibility of gaining or losing money (or sex.) Regardless of your own gender, you're probably at least aware of the basic behaviors and utter lack of intelligent decision-making ability when men are driven by primal desires and fears. Your ability to read the many aspects of this large market participants' intentions should transcend the question, "What will my opponents do next?" The better question for your to ask is, "What are my opponents wishing they could do?" Then you'll be taking his money home with you instead.

APPENDIX I
REVIEW OF THE BASICS

The basics of the FX markets are worth reviewing to clarify some of the misunderstandings and misconceptions spread by Forex marketing web sites on the internet.

What is the Forex Market?

The market for foreign exchange (or "Forex", "FX") is a global network of banking institutions who trade currencies with each other in a double auction market format. They determine the "exchange rates" of currencies, traditionally against the US Dollar, and subsequently against each other. If you're entirely new to the concept of a double auction market, the most commonly known examples are the stock exchanges where shares of public corporations are traded. The main difference, however, is that Forex has never been formally centralized.

The prices of currencies (exchange rates of any particular currency relative to a foreign "quote currency") move as a result of supply and demand. And yes, there is in fact a "price". The rate of the EUR/USD (Euro vs. US Dollar) currency pair is literally "the price of Euros, quoted in US Dollars." And from the perspective of the interbank market, the pair is indeed traded this way.

Why isn't there a single price? (Why is there a Bid-Ask Spread?)

Beginners are often confused, and maybe even disappointed, to find that there never seems to be one single price or exchange rate at any given time.

It doesn't help that non-traders often ask, "What's the Euro worth?" as though a single number could ever be the correct answer. While it's entirely possible to quote an average or an approximation, there is never one single price in Forex nor any other double auction market, including stocks, futures, etc. Why? Because the true market price is never the most recent transaction (aka. "Last" Price) - that, by definition, is the past.

The real market price, to you as a trader, is either the bid or the ask depending on whether you are currently a buyer or a seller.

If you are a potential buyer, then the price you can buy it at any given time is the ask price. If you are a potential seller, then the price you can sell it at any given time is the bid price.

In any double auction market, there will always be a "spread" - the difference between the bid and ask. This is not a new concept created by Forex brokers to cheat traders, it's a natural phenomenon of a double auction market. The reason "spreads" have become a profanity in the retail Forex market is because the traditional FX broker's business model is to widen the spread (and to collect the difference as a fee) rather than charge a commission as stock and futures brokers typically do. (The exception is the trend of "ECN" Forex brokers who stream a more transparent price and charge a commission instead. Either way, no broker will operate for free.)

The bid will always be lower, because by nature the bid is the highest price that others are currently willing to buy at (hence, the highest you can sell to immediately.) And the ask will always be higher because it's the lowest that others are willing to sell at (the lowest you can buy from immediately.) Any party that posts bids and asks are liquidity providers. If you are looking to buy immediately ("at market"; with "marketable orders") then you're a liquidity remover. Liquidity providers can be other traders or even large banks - though, in most cases, if you're a beginner who is starting off with a Micro or Mini account at a retail FX broker, your liquidity provider is your own broker. You can effectively act as a liquidity provider as well, but there may be limitations to this in FX depending on the structure of your broker. (Most brokers who offer micro or mini trade sizes can't allow direct access to larger participants because those entities simply won't trade with you at such insignificant sizes.) In effect, however, if you post limit orders of any kind, you are in a way acting as a liquidity provider; the only issue being that if you are trading with a dealer, your liquidity will only ever be removed if the broader market has moved past your price against you.

At any given time, in a highly liquid market such as the EUR/USD, you may see a quote such as 1.2304 bid / 1.2305 ask. What this means is that the highest price that your counterparties are willing to buy from you (for you to sell to) is 1.2304; the lowest price that they are willing to sell to you (for you to buy from) is 1.2305. The pip value on any non-JPY quoted pair is the fourth digit after the decimal point, so in this example, the bid is at 04 (with a 1.23 "big figure") and the ask is at 05 (with a 1.23 "big figure"). Therefore, a trader seeing this quote would say that there is a 1 pip spread.

Why are there Currency Pairs?

In the stock market, there is only one currency in which any given stock is officially priced. For example, the stock of GE (General Electric) listed on the New York Stock Exchange is quoted in US Dollars simply by nature of the fact that the NYSE is an American exchange. In the currency market, however, every currency can only be traded with another currency as the quote currency. For example, the price of GBP/USD (British Pound vs. US Dollar) is effectively the price of the British Pound, quoted in US Dollar. Likewise, the price of AUD/CAD (Australian Dollar vs. Canadian Dollar) could be seen as the price of an Australian Dollar quoted in Canadian Dollars.

In reality, the US Dollar had become the global reserve currency at the time the FX market became free-floating in the 1970's. (Prior to that, currencies had been pegged to gold, and even further back before World War II, the global reserve currency was the British Pound.) As a result, the USD pairs are often traded as the primary instruments of the FX market (for example, the question, "Where's the Euro today?" is typically referring to the price of the Euro relative to the US Dollar, aka. EUR/USD.) When a non-USD currency is paired with another non-USD currency, that's referred to as a cross rate or cross pair. (In spite of common misuse, a "cross" is not the same as a "pair" -- if the USD is involved and you refer to it as a cross, you've misunderstood the term regardless of what your opinion may be of the US Dollar as a reserve currency in the 21st century.)

What is a pip?

Currency pairs are traded in 1/100th of the lowest standard denomination of the quote currency. (The currency on the right side.) The lowest standard denomination of US Dollars is the penny (0.01) so 1/100th of that is 0.0001. The lowest denomination of the Japanese Yen is 1 (a single Yen is locally used in Japan as the equivalent of a penny, not a dollar) so the pip value for JPY-quoted pairs is 0.01.

Today, most of the FX market prices in fractions of a pip (or "sub-pips") but the proper definition of a pip is still 1/100th of the lowest physical denomination of each currency. That new digit (1/1000th) is roughly equivalent to the 0.1 cent (1/10th of a penny) pricing in US stocks. In other words, that last digit is there and it'll economically affect you when you trade... but no trader in their right mind will go around quoting that last digit in casual conversation about the daily open, high, low, and close prices; or support and resistance levels. (In fact, if the EUR/USD is at 1.45235 bid / 1.45242 ask, most FX day traders will simply see this as "23 by 24" with a "1.45" big figure. The last digits, 5 in the bid and 2 in the ask, won't stay long enough at most times of day to even quote it verbally in conversation.)

Why are JPY pairs quoted differently?

While the Japanese Yen may appear to be priced extremely low at all times, this is actual deceiving because the local use of the Yen within Japan itself - a highly developed advanced economy - is actually equivalent to a US cent, not a dollar. For instance, domestic (non-imported) Japanese films would realistically sell on DVD or Blu-Ray for approximately 1500 to 3500 Yen, not 15 to 35 Yen. The equivalent income of a person who would make $150,000 per year in the US would actually earn 15,000,000 Yen.

Therefore, in keeping with the rule that pips are 1/100th of the lowest denomination of the quote currency, JPY-quoted pairs' pip values appear at only two decimal places rather than four decimal places as with USD-quoted pairs.

The real "par value", or 1:1 price, of USD/JPY (one US Dollar priced in Japanese Yen) is 100.00, not 1.0000.

The Basics of Charting

The trading world is occasionally divided between those who swear by the chart (or some form of "technical analysis") and those who swear by fundamentals. In day trading and especially automated trading, there are also those who would even tell you that both are useless and only statistics matter. In any case, if you're a beginner to Forex or any other market, it's a good idea to familiarize yourself with the basic concepts of charting for financial instruments, even if you plan to use it only as a quick visualization tool - or maybe even as a way to see what the common traders might be seeing.

Whether you agree with its efficacy or not, charting is among the natural results of the human tendency to visualize things at every given opportunity, so learning to read them and understand them is an integral skill.

Here are the basics to reading a chart of historical data.

Japanese Candlesticks

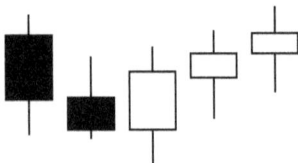

One of the most common types of charting in financial markets around the world are Japanese Candlestick charts.

Each candlestick represents historical price information in a specific period of time. For instance, if you've set your chart to "daily", then each of the candles represents one day. If you chose "5 minutes", then each candle represents five minutes.

Let's break down the basic information that each candle actually tells you:

The thick part of the candle is the body. The thin parts at the top and bottom are wicks. Candlestick charts always display each candle with a body in two possible colors. While these colors may vary (it may use green/red, blue/white, black/white, etc.) the important part to understand is that there is always only ever going to be two possible colors on each chart. In our examples, we've chosen black and white. If the body is black, it means that price was lower at the end of the period than the beginning. And vice versa for white. For example, if this is a daily chart, then a black candle represents a day on which price was lower at the close than at the open of the day. If this is a one hour chart, then price was lower at the end of the hour than at the beginning. So using the black and white example chart, the black bodied candles are periods when price closed lower than it opened (bear candle)

and the white bodied candles are periods when price closed higher than it opened (bull candle).

For a one-hour bear candle, the open price (first price at the beginning of the hour) is the top of the body, and the close price (last price of the hour) is the bottom of the body. The wick at the top reaches up to the high (the highest price that was reached during the hour); and the wick at the bottom reaches down to the low (the lowest price reached during the hour.) Conversely, for a bull candle (one that, by definition, closed higher than it opened, as signified by the color of its body -- in this case, white) the open price is the bottom of the body and the close price is the top of the body. The wicks, of course, retain the same meaning as they show the highest and lowest prices reached during the period in question.

OHLC Bars

The other most common charting style used by traders are OHLC Bar Charts (or simply "Bar Charts").

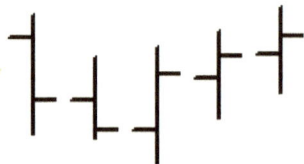

Like Japanese Candlesticks, OHLC bar charts show the historical open, high, low, and close prices of a given period.

Again, let's break down the information shown by each bar:

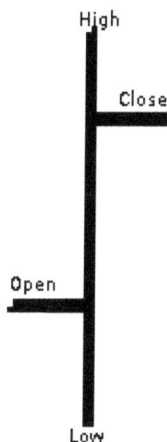

The basic concept of the bar chart is the same as a candlestick, except that a single thin line stretches from the low to the high at all times. The open and close of the bar is shown by a small line to the left (for the open) and another to the right (for the close).

There are other forms of charts, but most are less popular and typically convey far less specific information about historical price action. Line charts, for instance, fail to show much of the real price action within a time period.

Overall, the choice between candles and bars is a matter of personal preference and habit. The same information is shown on an OHLC Bar Chart as is shown on Japanese Candlestick charts. And most importantly, the same limitations and issues will arise no matter which one you choose on any given software package.

Limitations of Charts

While many traders who are past the beginner phase would probably skip the basic explanations of candles and bars, the limitations and issues associated with both types of charts should be reviewed. These are issues that may, at times, be taken for granted.

Firstly, charts are only able to show one specific type of pricing information. In stocks, the choice is between bid, ask, or last. The important one being "last", meaning the last price at which a stock was actually transacted. In the Forex market, there is no reliable equivalent to a chart of "last" prices simply because there is no centralized reporting system for transactions. FX charts can only accurately display historical bids alone, or historical asks alone.

While this limitation may appear trivial (and if your trading style involves long-term position trades, then this is actually a trivial matter) day traders will find that the highs and lows may at times be misleading due to the spread between the actual bid and ask prices. In some cases, your charting software may provide the option to show ask charts, but the vast majority of retail FX platforms are actually displaying bid prices only.

This, in itself, is not a major problem but traders should keep this limitation in mind and compensate accordingly. For example, if the pair you are trading averages a spread of about 2 to 4 pips, then allow for an extra 2 to 4 pips at the high of each candle or bar. Depending on your trading style, this may or may not be a major issue but always be sure to be aware of this if you're using the chart as a gauge of highs and lows of a recent period.

The second issue with charts is that they often tend to lull traders into a false perception of predictive potential. In other words, by seeing patterns where there may or may not be, people often begin to believe they can predict the future more accurately than they realistically will by simply observing the recent data in chart form. Remember, charts are just visualizations of historical data. That's not necessarily a weakness, but keep in mind that that's all they ever will be. They're not magic crystal balls. If you have a statistical reason to believe something may happen more likely after a certain pattern that occurred in the recent past, then you're free to backtest it and check it against a larger set of historical data. Just don't assume that it can tell you anything for an absolute fact beyond informing you of something that's already happened.

Lastly, there are countless technical indicators available for charting on any given market. There are also snake oil salesmen willing to take your money to convince you that some magical combination of them will attain infinite profits for you if only you follow a specific set of rules using indicators. If this were true, hundreds of millions of institutional capital on Wall Street would be pouring into funding automated trading systems that did nothing but follow technical indicator signals. If it were that simple, why would any institution bother with quantitative traders who spend hours developing statistical analysis based methods?

The problem is not the technical indicators; the problem is the way in which they are often misused as magic crystal balls.

As retail Forex traders began to mature, a movement of sorts has hit the internet's Forex trading community: A rebound against the initial wave of individual trader education material that adhered strictly to technical analysis using indicators as buy and sell signals. This new wave came along and advocated nothing but "naked trading" - as in, trading with no indicators, using raw price action alone.

While this price action trading rebound was well-meaning and has arguably proved to help many beginners and struggling traders take a few steps forward in seeing the market action in a more grounded perspective, it's also worth taking a critical look at the drawbacks of this phenomenon.

Remember, technical indicators are simply mathematical derivatives of historical price data... and so are OHLC bars and candlesticks. Indicators, bars, and candles are all derivatives of price based on the open, high, low, and close prices of an arbitrary period of time. The only difference is: Technical indicators derive their values from the data already shown by bars and candles, so they are an extra step of calculations. Still, that doesn't necessarily make them universally useless.

Moving averages, MACD, RSI, Stochastic Oscillators, and other popular indicators are all generated by mathematical formulas using open, high, low, and close historical price data - even if that "historical" refers to one minute ago or one tick ago. Sometimes, they're even able to output what appears to be artful displays of that data which leads beginner traders into believing that the indicator has more predictive ability than it really does about what's to come on the hard right edge of the chart. The indicator's output is not the problem; the trader's potential misinterpretation of its significance is what might cause problems.

The truth is that technical indicators are simply an alternative means of looking at past market prices, whether it's a long time ago or two milliseconds ago. And that's not necessarily a bad thing for a trader to look at. The key ingredient is that you should familiarize yourself with the actual mathematical formula used to calculate the values generated by an indicator. Never choose an indicator simply because your favorite educator recommends it; or because you randomly chose it when you installed your trading software. Almost every known technical indicator is extensively documented in books or the internet with explanations of their original concepts and, most importantly, the exact formula used to calculate its output values. Get to know it, understand it, and honestly assess whether it will help you when you look at recent price data. Always remember that no formula can possibly tell the future, but if it can portray the past in a way that helps you more quickly assess what recently happened in the market - and if that information helps in your particular trading method - then go ahead and use it.

If you're going to arm yourself with a tool that will affect your trading income, be sure you know that tool intimately, inside and out. Never take anything at face value.

Indicators are not unique in that the only objective price information available to most market participants (aside from the current bid and ask prices) is data from the past. "Naked traders" who trade based on price action alone are effectively doing the same thing: interpreting historical price data. Neither "naked traders" nor indicator-based traders are actually seeing any form of objective data from the future. It's just a matter of using the available information from the past to augment your decisions about that future. Depending on your circumstances and your proficiency as a trader, using a combination of the skills from both philosophies of trading may be more constructive than adhering to only one or the other religiously.

Once you've become familiar with the details of an indicator, you have the opportunity to observe the indicator's output "behavior" patterns. For instance, one indicator might spike more violently on a first break-out of a range than others. If these sorts of visualizations are helpful to you in some way, then by all means use it.

Just remember what these tools are objectively capable of, and consider that what works for you may not always be what all of your peers in the business currently agree with. Some of the greatest accomplishments in humanity have been accomplished by people who did the opposite of prevailing wisdom in the time and place they lived. By all means, learn the weaknesses and strengths of every tool you come across - regardless of their reputation among the community at large - and master the ones that work for you.

In the end, it doesn't matter what every other trader on the planet thinks of any of the tools you choose to utilize. If any tool in the world helps you make money with limited and controlled risk, then don't let anyone stop you from continuing with exactly what you're doing.

APPENDIX II
FOREX TERMS

Glossary of common terms, and terms used throughout this book, related to trading in the FX markets.

A-Book - A broker's customer trades which are passed on to their liquidity providers in terms of exposure. For example, if Customer A buys one lot of EUR/USD from the broker, and the broker (typically via an automated system) immediately transmits the equivalent one-lot buy trade with their liquidity providers. This trade was a proper A-Book trade. There is no conflict of interest between the broker and the customer in such a trade.

Ask - The lowest price that your counterparties are willing to sell to you. In FX trading platforms, this is typically the default price at which you can buy (or buy to cover a short).

B-Book - Unlike an A-Book trade, these are held on the broker's own books. In other words, the broker does not transmit an equivalent trade to a liquidity provider, and therefore the broker's exposure to the trade is in direct conflict of interest with the customer. If the customer wins this trade, the broker loses, and vice versa.

Base Currency - The currency on the left side of the symbol name. Example: On the EUR/USD, EUR (Euro) is the base currency.

Bid - The highest price that your counterparties are willing to buy from you. In FX trading platforms, this is typically the default price at which you can sell or short sell.

Com Dolls - The "Commodity Dollar Pairs" or "Commodity Pairs" are USD/CAD (US Dollar vs. Canadian Dollar), AUD/USD (Australian Dollar vs. US Dollar), and NZD/USD (New Zealand Dollar vs. US Dollar). The term originates from the fact that the currencies of Australia, New Zealand, and Canada are heavily correlated with commodities such as gold, agricultural commodities, and crude oil.

Cross Pairs - Cross pairs or cross rates refers to any currency pair that does not involve the US Dollar. In the post-World War II era, the US Dollar became the global reserve currency and all foreign exchange trading revolved around the USD. While the global reserve currency status of the US Dollar has long been under threat in the 21st century, the FX market remains a product of the post-WWII era and the term "cross" continues to refer exclusively to any currency pair that does not involve the USD. For example, EUR/GBP (Euro vs. British Pound) is a cross pair. (Specifically, one lot of EUR/GBP is the cross rate of one lot of EUR/USD and the inverse of GBP/USD divided by the current value of GBP/USD). Beginners often misuse the term "cross" as a synonym for "pair" but the two terms have very distinct meanings. While this may appear to be a technicality, confusion of these terms can lead beginners to a drastic misunderstanding of many news items or comments by advanced traders involving "the crosses".

ECN - An acronym used throughout finance for "Electronic Communications Network". For all practical purposes, an ECN is an automated order matching system that eliminates the need for human intervention in matching buyers and sellers. In the FX markets, the term ECN typically refers to any system that may connect traders to other traders or connect traders to the dealer's liquidity providers. The emphasis is on the lack of a need for a human dealer's involvement and the purpose is typically to eliminate the conflict of interest between a dealer and a trader by matching orders against other participants (either directly or using an automated exposure offset system of some sort.)

Forex - Short for "Foreign Exchange". Also shortened as "FX". The term refers to the exchange of foreign currencies and has never been intended to connote a centralized exchange of any kind. Unlike the markets for stocks (equities), futures contracts, bonds (fixed income), and other similar financial instruments, the FX market has never been centralized and has always operated as a loosely connected network of banks and financial institutions. Nevertheless, the increasing number of liquidity aggregation systems and mere price competition (and arbitrage opportunities created by any differences in pricing) tend to keep the pricing quoted by different parties in FX relatively close to each other in spite of the decentralized nature of the market.

Limit Order - Any order that will only be executed at its limit price or better. (All limit orders, by definition, must include a limit price.)

Liquidity - Liquidity is usually defined as the ability to convert an asset into cash. In the markets, the real use of the term -- while technically consistent with the original definition -- is more accurately described as the amount of opportunity offered by other participants to convert your position back to your account's base currency. For instance, if you are long EUR/GBP in a USD-denominated trading account, the amount of bids and offers (active limit orders) on the market for EUR/GBP are your opportunities to convert your position in EUR/GBP back to your account's USD balance. Because you can only buy from or sell to active limit orders, limit orders are effectively the available liquidity. When trading against a single counterparty such as a Forex dealer, the dealer's willingness to buy or sell at a specific price is your liquidity

(the dealer, in this case, acts as sole liquidity provider, although they may in many cases be offsetting their trades immediately against larger interbank market participants.)

Long Position - A position that is opened with a buy order to be closed later at a profit or loss with a sell order. Effectively, a long position is a bet on the rise of a financial asset's value.

Lot - Traditionally, one lot in FX is 100,000 units of base currency. In some rare cases, a platform targeted toward professional traders may define a lot as 1 Million units of base currency. Likewise, some platforms targeting beginners may set one lot as 10,000 units of base currency. (If nothing else is specified, the traditional definition in the FX markets is 100,000 units of base currency.) This term is the FX equivalent to similar concepts used in other markets such as on U.S. stock exchanges, where one lot is 100 shares.

Major Pairs - The major pairs are traditionally considered to be the most heavily traded USD denominated pairs. EUR/USD (Euro vs. US Dollar, which effectively took the place of the Deutschemark vs. US Dollar as the most heavily traded currency pair in the FX markets), GBP/USD (British Pound vs. US Dollar), USD/JPY (US Dollar vs. Japanese Yen), and USD/CHF (US Dollar vs. Swiss Franc) are the four major pairs. While opinions may vary about any or all of the currencies involved, the fact remains that these pairs are the most liquid and transact the highest volume on a daily basis in the FX markets as of the early 21st century. Whether this continues to be the case or not, the term "major pairs" will likely continue to refer to these four pairs.

Margin - Collateral used to support open positions when trading on leverage. FX is typically traded on leverage, and the collateral typically consists of the cash balance and the mark-to-market value of currently open positions in the account.

Market Order - Any order that is entered to be executed at the prevailing market price (buy from the counterparty's offer or sell to the counterparty's bid). Market orders, by definition, do not specify a specific price and therefore may experience slippage depending on the amount of liquidity available on the market at any given time.

MetaTrader - One of the most popular FX trading platforms available to individual traders.

MQL - MetaQuotes Language, the programming language used by the MetaTrader platform.

Pair - Currency pairs are the instruments traded

in the FX market. (Currencies can only be traded against another currency.) Pair may also refer to pair trading, a specific type of statistical arbitrage trading strategy in which two instruments (such as two different companies' stocks) are paired against each other with a long position on one stock hedged by a short position in the other stock.

Pip - On most currency pairs, the pip value is the 4th digit after the decimal place. (For example, in the price 1.23258, the "5" is the pip value and this price may commonly be referred to as "25" when traders reference it during a trading session.) For Japanese Yen (JPY) quoted pairs such as USD/JPY or GBP/JPY, the 2nd digit after the decimal place is the pip value. This is due to the local usage (within Japan) of a single unit of Yen as the equivalent to a cent rather than a dollar. Note: Regardless of whether your FX broker quotes using an extra decimal place or not (5 digits after the decimal place on most pairs; 3 digits after the decimal on JPY pairs), the pip value will always refer to the 4th for most pairs (2nd for JPY pairs). The last digit in such cases is commonly referred to as a "sub pip" or "fractional pip". Occasionally, it may be referred to as a "point". A major cause of confusion began when many MetaTrader brokers switched to quoting with an extra digit and the software incorrectly referred to the new final digit as a pip value.

Quote - A quote on any financial market consists of a bid and an ask.

Quote Currency - The currency on the right side of the symbol name. Example: On the EUR/USD, USD (US Dollar) is the quote currency.

Rollover - Traditionally, in the FX market, all open positions are "rolled over" at the close of New York business hours in order for rollover rates to be charged and/or credited to the trader for the positions held. These rollover rates are factors of the differences between the interest rates of the two countries involved in the currency pair.

Short Position - A position that is opened with a sell order to be closed later at a profit or loss with a buy (buy to cover) order. Effectively, a short position is a bet on the fall of a financial asset's value.

Slippage - Sudden changes in the bid and ask may occur between the time a trader enters a market order and the time that order is filled. For instance, if there are 5 million standing on the offer and a trader places a buy (at market) order, all 5 million may have been consumed by other traders prior to this order hitting the market (some or all of the 5 million may also be cancelled at any time by the participant who posted the offers.) The result is slippage: the trader will received a worse price than the price quoted at the time of order entry. Slippage is a perfectly natural phenomenon in any real market. However, in a natural market environment, slippage may be either positive or negative to the trader -- not only negative. An ethical issue only arises when a dealer deliberately allows only negative slippage to impact a customer (but never positive slippage) and this issue tends to distort many individual FX traders' impression of slippage as a phenomenon in itself.

Spread - The difference between the bid and ask price. Regardless of whether you are trading against a dealer or on an ECN with interbank participants, the quote will always consist of a bid and an ask because they are respectively the highest price participants are currently willing to buy at; and the lowest price other participants are willing to sell at. The difference is the "spread" which would be your hypothetical cost of entry and exit at any given time using market orders. While FX dealers may determine their spreads, spreads in and of themselves are not an artificial part of any market.

STP - In the retail FX markets, STP refers to "Straight Through Processing", a method of order processing used by brokers and dealers to automatically offset the dealer's exposure and effectively eliminate the need for human dealer intervention in accepting or rejecting orders from traders. Along with ECN, the concept of STP became a popular structure offered by FX dealers following the backlash against the traditional human dealing desk business model which created numerous conflict of interest issues between the dealer and the customer.

Trading Platform - Common term for a trading software package used by traders to place orders and keep track of open positions.

ABOUT THE AUTHOR

J.T. Wellesley worked as a dealer on the trading desk of a retail Forex brokerage for two years following more than a decade of experience in the U.S. commodity futures, fixed income, and equities markets. Today, Wellesley contributes editorials with an alternative perspective on the global currency markets to various finance-related social media outlets and manages a private capital portfolio in currencies and equity options.

Forex Day Trading Exposed